Westward Ho!

My Life in America

Brenda Wallis Smith

Author of *A Pennine Childhood*

ISBN: 0692063307
ISBN 13: 9780692063309

To my dear husband,
Joseph Victor Smith,
with love.

Contents

CHAPTER 1

Westward Ho!

ONE SEPTEMBER MORNING IN 1951, a fortnight after we were married in a parish church in our English village, Joe and I arrived in New York Harbor. Joe was on deck, leaning on the ship's rail, taking in the magnificent views of lower Manhattan, the New York skyline, the Statue of Liberty, and exulting over what he thought of as the beginning of an exciting adventure. Meanwhile, I was below in our cabin, puking up my breakfast. I'd been doing this ever since the *Mauritania* left the quiet waters off Portsmouth, on the south coast of England, and hit the turbulent thirty-foot waves of the Atlantic. Even after I managed to stagger up the stairs to where Joe was standing, I was too busy swallowing hard to take much note of my surroundings.

Traveling to America was not what I'd imagined I'd be doing when I first began going out with Joe Smith from Barn Close Farm. We'd both grown up in the small village of Fritchley, Derbyshire, a steep ribbon of a place that stretches from the height of The Tors, a stony ridge at the top of the village, down a twisting road that ends at a small stream in the valley. I lived up; Joe lived down. World War II loomed over much of our childhood with the Luftwaffe flying overhead, and the threat of bombs. Joe's father was a member of the Home Guard that protected our local reservoirs; four of my uncles and a cousin served in the British Armed Forces. Only the cousin did not return. Food was heavily rationed throughout wartime and was not lifted until 1956. It took a month to save up sufficient sugar for my mother to make a birthday cake.

The *Mauritania* was a revelation. During the war that magnificent vessel had been a troop ship, its furniture, wood paneling, bars, and restaurants ripped out to make room for the thousands of troops who were to be shipped with their weapons to Europe and the East. However, after Victory in Japan (V-J Day, August 15, 1945), it had been completely remodeled, and our cabin seemed the height of luxury, as did the stateroom, the library, the swimming pool, and the cinema. We had been forced to reserve cabin class with these amenities, because other young job seekers had already filled steerage. The luxury of our midlevel berth meant that the food was glamorous: oranges and bananas, which we and our fellow Britons hadn't seen since 1939; real eggs, not that awful wartime powdered stuff; white bread, which today I never allow to pass my lips. All this in addition to Butter! Chocolate! Cream!

We began our journey from Portsmouth full of excitement. With the smell of the briny in our nostrils and the wind in our hair, we strode the decks, feeling like Vikings venturing toward an unknown land.

Unfortunately, the minute we hit the open Atlantic, I discovered that my heart was made not of oak but of plywood; Sir Francis Drake would have had me walk the plank. I was no sailor, and neither the ship nor I stopped heaving until the foghorns began bellowing and the sea became less turbulent off the misty coast of Newfoundland. Traveling south down the New England coast, the waves again grew high, and I regained my feet only just in time to join Joe and lean feebly against the ship's railing as we nosed slowly up the Hudson River to Pier 90.

And thus began my sixty years in America: a time of fascinating work and great success for my husband, the births of our two daughters, and, for myself, deep homesickness for England, excitement at the beauties of the American landscape, and my acceptance of my new homeland as we passed through the Civil Rights Era of the 1950s and 1960s with the assassinations of American President John F. Kennedy in 1963 and civil-rights leader Dr. Martin Luther King in 1968; the Vietnam War and the anti-war movement; and the burgeoning women's movement in the late 1960s and the early 1970s. At the same time, there was Joe's work for NASA on the moon rocks and a life lived in Chicago; Washington, DC; Cambridge, England; Pennsylvania; Los Angeles; and Boston. Going West has been the adventure of my life.

CHAPTER 2

Courting

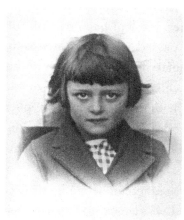

JOE AND I MET at Fritchley School, in Derbyshire. I was eight, tall for my age, round faced, with short, dark hair, cut with a fringe across my forehead. I noticed Joe particularly because he was among the few of my fellow students who were not put off by what they called my "posh" accent. Real Fritchleyites "talked broad." Like me he was eight, a little light-haired fellow dressed in gray wool pants that came just below his knees to be met by thick socks. For his walk to school, he had a tweed jacket and a flat cap.

Joe was the eldest son of a farming family with deep roots in the area. His forebears had moved to the neighboring village,

Crich, in the early eighteen hundreds, from their homestead just seven miles away near Ashover, Derbyshire. In Crich the family included farmers, butchers, blacksmiths, joiners, and the owner of a pub.

After our time together at Fritchley Church of England School, we lost track of each other. Joe had been one of only two students at Fritchley who had passed an exam known as the "Eleven-Plus" and won a free scholarship to Strutt's Grammar School in nearby Belper. Meanwhile, I and the rest of our cohorts at Fritchley C of E failed the exam, after which I applied to Ernest Bailey's Secondary School in Matlock, where my mother's family, the Durwards, lived. My parents would have to pay fees.

I didn't see Joe again until I was nineteen, when he showed up at the library in Belper where I was working. By that time, he was a handsome young fellow of nineteen, his light-colored hair now a rich brown, his eyes either very blue or very green, which depended on the color of his shirt. He was also very clever and had been the only student in Derbyshire at the time to win a scholarship to Cambridge University. He invited me out.

Since the age of seventeen, Joe had been busy with his classes at the university. At the time, most Cambridge students were rich and upper class, which made it hard for a work-ing-class boy to be accepted. He was able to make a few friends among lower-class students, but it was a long time before he felt he was part of the student body. He told me about an episode with one of the "upper-class twits," who made denigrating remarks about his Derbyshire accent. The boy was standing at the foot of a staircase that led to their dorm rooms in Caius College. He had a trunk with him. In response to the student's jibes, Joe seized the trunk, carried it rapidly up one set of stairs, then up another that branched off in a different direction, and dumped it outside the wrong room. I could imagine him brushing his hands together triumphantly, as he descended the stairs. Sometimes it pays to have spent one's youth hauling hay onto the stack.

Both sets of parents were happy about our impending marriage, mine because my mother had feared that because I was twenty-three and still unmarried, I would turn out to be an old maid. And as for Joe's parents, Mrs. Smith told my mother that she and her husband were "glad it's your Brenda, Mrs. Wallis, and not one of those foreigners from Cambridge."

Joe and I had begun "courting," as it was called, when we were both nineteen, and agreed to marry when we were both turning twenty-three, during his last year at Cambridge. He was awarded his PhD that year, and shortly thereafter we were married.

Having been cajoled by a schoolmate at Fritchley, I had joined the local Primitive Methodists, and consequently had no knowledge of Church of England practices. I left the choice of wedding hymns to Joe's mother. She informed me that we would sing, "We Plough the Fields and Scatter," no doubt chosen in honor of Joe's farming heritage, and the Navy hymn, "Eternal Father," which has

the refrain "Oh hear us when we cry to thee / For those in peril on the sea." I wondered if her choice of the latter indicated that she feared the *Mauritania* might sink.

Although plans for our marriage had been (somewhat) under our control, Joe's job-hunting was full of problems. While he had been at university, soldiers who had been away fighting the Nazis began to come home; consequently, all the positions in Britain, at least in the scientific world, were filled. In desperation Joe looked into an offer from Cadbury's, the chocolate manufacturers in Yorkshire, who needed scientific help with their formulae. This proved to be too far out of his (geologic) field, although the access to unending chocolate was enticing.

A university in Uruguay offered a position with a salary of $3,000 a year, a princely sum in those days. We both voted no; to us, Uruguay was unknown territory and, according to Joe, not in the forefront of scientific research. Then a friend told us about an Australian scheme in which young Britons who qualified were being offered steamer tickets to Down Under for ten pounds, then the equivalent of roughly twenty-eight US dollars. However, no jobs accompanied the tickets, which could have left us jobless and a long way from home. As in England, returning troops had already filled any positions available at Australian universities, and so Joe didn't become what the Aussies labeled "a ten-pound Pom." (The scheme lasted until 1970.)

Fortunately, at this point an American professor named Frank Tuttle turned up in Cambridge, trolling for postdocs: students who had just completed their PhDs. He offered Joe a three-year position with the Geophysical Laboratory, part of the Carnegie Institution of Washington, DC, and we decided to join the so-called "Brain Drain": young people, almost always men, with various degrees who opted to cross the Atlantic for work. The salary offered was $1,000, much less than Uruguay's $3,000, but the language would be English (sort of), and in any case, we were both interested in experiencing the land we thought we knew after hours spent at the Hay Barn, a local movie house in the nearby village of Crich.

And so Joe and I were married, spent a week's honeymoon at Torquay on the south coast of England, went back home to Derbyshire, bought suitcases and a cabin trunk, packed our few wartime "utility" clothes and sparse wedding presents—the shops were still bare of goods—said tearful good-byes to our families, and at last were ready to set sail for the West.

CHAPTER 3

First Impressions

IN NEW YORK, AS Joe and I made our way through US Customs, I made my first transatlantic mistake: confessing I had wedding presents with me. America immediately robbed me of what seemed a great deal of money: an import tax that was then the equivalent of eight pounds. After paying for our train tickets, this left us with only seven dollars to travel from New York to Washington, DC, a journey of over two hundred miles, not to mention start our new life!

Our taxi driver, probably spotting a couple of rubes, suggested he show us the skyscrapers, especially the Empire State Building, on our way to Grand Central Station. I admitted the famous landmark was tall, but the streets were crowded and dark among all those gigantic structures and echoed with the shuffle of hundreds of feet, the growl and blat of car engines, the roar of motorbikes, the blare of police cars and ambulances. I was not impressed.

In the vast cavern that was Grand Central Station, we were puzzled to find no trains, and Joe left me to protect the luggage while he went to investigate. Long after I had begun to fear that American gangsters had rubbed him out, Joe at last came back to assure me that our train was waiting for us underground, and that he'd seen no bad guys. Had the films I'd enjoyed at our local cinema skewed my view of America?

As we traveled through the dark night, the journey to Washington, DC, revealed brilliantly lit parking lots full of enormous cars, followed by something that resembled the burning ghats of India: acres of what I now suppose must have been flares produced by oil refineries along the coast. After what was to me a long and troubled journey—the conductor locked the toilets every time we approached a station, and sometimes forgot to unlock them—we arrived in Washington around midnight, and to my vast relief found Joe's American contact, Frank Tuttle, waiting for us on the platform.

Frank was a tall, friendly, cheerful fellow with a huge grin, his large skull decorated by fair curly hair. After he and Joe had retrieved our luggage and stowed it, cabin trunk and all, into the enormous boot of his car, he drove us out to the Maryland suburb where we were to be his guests until we could find somewhere to live. Frank's wife and two young children were in their beds by the time we arrived; exhausted, we tumbled into ours, our slumbers only vaguely disturbed by a cacophony of frogs from a nearby marsh.

The next morning, we met our hostess, a friendly, blonde woman who, after I had addressed her as Mrs. Tuttle, insisted that we use first names.

"Call me Don," she said.

"*Don*?" said I. "Why, in England Donald's a man's name!"

My ear for American pronunciation was also not as sharp as I'd supposed.

This seemingly older woman, whose name I finally realized was Dawn, couldn't have been a day over thirty, but seemed as much a figure of authority as my mother.

The Tuttle's house was in one of the new developments that had sprung up around Washington after the war, when a severe housing shortage became critical as servicemen and women began to flood home from overseas. It was a two-story redbrick detached house with, on the first floor, a large living room, a kitchen, and a small room Frank used as an office and that doubled as our bedroom. Off the hall a small room held a toilet, washbasin, and a shower, which I decided would make me cleaner than the baths I'd had to share with my sister when fuel for hot water was scarce in wartime Britain.

Upstairs was another bathroom and three bedrooms. The kitchen was not as large as the one at my parents' house in Fritchley, but it had gleaming white-tiled walls, and appliances that my mother could only dream about: a washing machine, a dryer, a dishwasher, and a huge refrigerator. (At Ballantrae House, we were reduced to keeping our foodstuffs in a space under the stairs). At the back of the house, a pleasant garden with a flagged patio was visible from the living-room windows; however, the "open plan" at the front of the house consisted of a lawn with only a few low bushes near the door and not a flower border in sight. I was astonished: with no fences or hedges to differentiate the Tuttle's lawn from their neighbors', how did they know which was theirs? How did they protect their privacy? Who mowed what? America was turning out to be a puzzle.

As soon as the lushness of the Tuttle's appliances and abundance of food began to wear off, I found just how dull a suburb could be, especially a new one. There were no shops, no sidewalks, no parks, and so nowhere to walk; just street upon street of identical redbrick houses, most of them in dead straight rows with here and there a few curved ones. This meant that every morning after Frank and Joe had driven away to work at the Geophysical Lab, the children had left for school, and Dawn was at her teaching job, there was virtually nothing for me to do but stack a few dishes in the dishwasher and take myself off to the bedroom to read, or to write letters home. This was when I decided that I would never again live in a suburb.

One Saturday, Dawn, probably having realized my isolation, invited some of her women friends for coffee. She introduced me to them—coyly, I felt—as "a new bride." At this there was a stir among the guests and they all turned to look at me, all of them cooing, "Oh, gee! A bride!" I felt my face redden. These people were more sentimentally inclined than this Northern Brit, and I began to wonder why I'd allowed myself to be whisked off to such an alien land. It was not at all how I had imagined it.

CHAPTER 4

Our First Home

DESPITE THE TUTTLE'S KINDNESS, Joe and I were happy when Frank came home with news of an apartment available not too far from the Lab, and suggested we take a look at it before someone else snapped it up. The flat, at 1615 Kenyon Street, NW, had one bedroom, a kitchen, a bathroom and a living room, plus an enormous walk-in closet. Newly divorced and wanting someone to take over his lease, the man who was renting the apartment stipulated that anyone who did so must buy his furniture as well. It seemed that apartments were in such short supply that even incumbent renters could bargain with incomers if, like we, they were green enough to allow it.

I thought the furniture adequate, if a trifle sparse, and suspected the renter's wife had taken the best of it. The bedroom had a double bed, its headboard made of light-colored wood, probably pine, a chest of drawers, and a matching dressing table with curved edging and the then-fashionable three swing mirrors. The living room was graced with a large green sofa, a matching armchair, and a "dinette set" in chrome with a red vinyl top and four matching chairs. The kitchen held a sink, a small refrigerator, a tiny table, and a two-way hatch into which we put our daily bag of garbage to be collected each morning by the janitor. There was no garbage disposal like that at the Tuttle's, so we put all our table scraps in a paper bag. This odiferous container soon made us aware of residents we hadn't bargained for: roughly four million cockroaches that squirmed over the kitchen walls every night. Thus we became the proud renters of our first apartment.

The five-story, redbrick building sat close to Massachusetts Avenue at the end of a tramline, where a vast turntable enlivened our days and nights with the shriek of metal-on-metal as the cars were turned around for their journey back to town. From the opposite direction, if the winds were westerly, we could hear lions roaring in the National Zoo on the other side of Rock Creek Park. The area was lower middle class where people worked in offices or shops in minor capacities, and lived in apartments or small bungalows. A few shops were strung along the street, although the most convenient way to fill our tiny fridge was to trek over to a store on Wisconsin Avenue, close to the Lab. This was a big thrill: my first-ever supermarket. Rationing, at least for us, was over. It would continue well into the fifties in Britain, after American "Lend/Lease" turned toward the Continent in order to feed the millions of homeless and starving people of Europe.

Across Massachusetts Avenue from our apartment lay what was then called the "ghetto," with its black population, and the theater where President Lincoln was murdered. Innocently, we walked there to inspect that historic building, not at first noticing that we were the only white people on the streets. No one harassed us, and I felt no fear, although when I stopped to admire two enchanting small children, all black curls and huge dark eyes, their mother corralled them as though she thought them to be in danger.

Unlike life in the Maryland suburb, we found many things to interest us in the city, and like the tourists we were, we visited the Capitol; admired the White House through its railings—it was open to the public only on special occasions; walked down the long, green Mall to view the Washington, Lincoln, and Jefferson Monuments; and visited various museums, including the Smithsonian and the National Gallery. In spring, the garden near the Mall was pink and sweet with apple blossom.

We took the streetcar downtown to attend chamber music concerts in the Capitol Rotunda, and later to the bank of the Potomac River where the symphony orchestra played on a floating arena moored close to shore. These were my first encounters with classical music—the beginning of a love that grew over the years. Before this, during World War II, I'd loved Bing Crosby's crooning: ba ba ba boooo, and big band music, such as that of Glenn Miller. During the War, I had been listening to a BBC broadcast of his band, when the music stopped, followed by the announcement that Miller's plane had been shot down by the Luftwaffe as he flew over the English Channel to give a concert for the troops. (My father asked, "What the dickens is Bren blubbing about now?" He was unaware of my worship of several wartime heroes.)

Joe and I also went to plays put on by students at Georgetown University, and took long rambles on the towpath beside the canal. Our favorite haunt was a path through the meadows and woods of Rock Creek Park that curled for miles around the city. Spring comes early to Washington, and it was warm even in February when early daffodils came into bloom, a golden cloud under the trees.

We had visitors, including William Scott MacKenzie—known to his friends as Mac—whom we had met back in Cambridge when he visited the Cavendish Lab where Joe was doing postgraduate work. Mac, born in Edinburgh, was already a lecturer at Manchester University. He owned a car, a convertible with a sunroof, and I felt very lofty as he drove us around the streets of Cambridge with the top down. When they came to Washington, Mac and his wife, Anne, rented an apartment on Wisconsin Avenue close to the Lab; although both were English, they had recently been married in Worcester, Massachusetts.

Another visitor was an old Cambridge friend of Joe's, a Welshman named Sam Edwards. He later became an adviser to the British government in matters scientific, and eventually earned a title: Sir Sam. He stayed with us in our one-bedroom apartment, and slept on the living room couch. I was afraid our friend might think this, lèse-majesté, but Sam was not a proud chap.

After we moved to Washington, I saw less of the Tuttles, although Joe continued to see Frank every day at the Lab. Dawn had two little girls to raise and taught something called "home economics" at a local college. "Why don't they call it housework and have done with it?" I said indignantly to Joe. "Do they really have to go to school to learn how to dust the piano?" (I can only say, with heartfelt relief, that I never voiced my juvenile opinions of American life to anyone American.)

CHAPTER 5

Back to Work

AS SOON AS WE were settled in our apartment, I began to look for a job. I was restless, and Joe's $1,000 a year, which seemed an enormous sum when we were informed of it in England, proved to be a little less than princely. I first tried the local library and was told I should apply to their headquarters downtown. I did so, feeling supremely confident.

After leaving school, I had applied for a position as a Junior at the Derby County Library headquarters and subsequently worked in every department, developing skills in cataloging and classification, and the use of the American Dewey Decimal System. This was in addition to the everyday jobs of a librarian: shelving returned books, advising the more educated about what was available in biography and history, steering old ladies toward what they called their "luuvv boooks," and finding Westerns and other such tales for the old gentlemen. I worked there for seven years, and during the final two, I was given charge of a traveling library that covered the western areas of Derbyshire.

During that time, I took various British Library Association courses in librarianship at the college in Derby and passed them without difficulty, but none of this cut any ice with the American Library Association. I was told I would have to start at the bottom again and go to an American library school. I was indignant.

There was no money for school, and in any case, I was reluctant to relearn what I told myself, no doubt mistakenly, I already knew.

Next, I tried the phone company. I rather fancied myself as a "Hello girl"; not a lady of doubtful morals, but one of those women I had seen in old black-and-white movies, working at banks of phones and cooing, "Number, please?" I was told my accent was "too British." Then I thought of trying the British Embassy where I could probably have landed a gofer job had I persevered. However, the sentry at the front gate intimidated me—I remember him wearing a busby hat, so instead of finding the tradesman's entrance, I crept away home.

By evening on job-expedition days, I was exhausted. I had only one pair of shoes suitable for wearing in town: the blue sandals I had worn to my wedding. The sole was coming loose on one of them, and each night I smeared it with glue in the hope that it would hold for another day. The repair usually lasted an hour or two, but the shoe was always coming apart again by the time I limped home.

After a month spent searching, I was successful at last after I spotted an ad for a receptionist at a company named Rynex and Saxon, a short tram ride down Massachusetts Avenue from our apartment. I had no idea what Rynex and Saxon produced, but was sure that being a receptionist was something I could do. With hopes high, I dressed for my interview in my best knee-length skirt, of which I had two, a blouse with the fashionable tie at the neck, a buttoned-up cardigan, and nylons. I was no bobby-soxer; I had spent my school and war years wearing rayon stockings held up by suspenders attached to a garment called a "liberty bodice." However, I was aware that American GIs had wooed older girls with nylon stockings, hence my choice. Mine were still held up with suspenders attached to a liberty bodice, but they had seams down the back, which made me kid myself I looked elegant.

At Rynex and Saxon, an old, liver-spotted gentleman interviewed me briefly—Mr. Saxon, it turned out—who immediately offered me the job. It was then I discovered that the firm's business was making false teeth.

I began work the following morning, and was given a small desk in a corner of Mr. Saxon's office, which was attached to the factory building, where thirty or more men were employed and the real work of the company was done. Mr. Saxon's role seemed mainly ornamental; Mr. Rynex was the boss. He was younger than his partner, and when I saw him, he was usually rushing in or out of the adjacent factory with a magnifying glass bobbing on his forehead and a fistful of false teeth in his hand. That first morning, he was dashing by when Mr. Saxon grabbed his arm and introduced us; Mr. Rynex raised his magnifying glass to me as if it were a hat, said "Hi," and rushed off again. That was the only time we spoke during the three months I was employed by Rynex and Saxon.

My closest colleague, a blonde secretary of about my age, kept me entertained during lunchtime with narration about the ups and downs of her affair with a policeman. Mr. Powers, a middle-aged Englishman, was the company's deliveryman. When he came to collect his instructions for the day, he would place one buttock on Mr. Saxon's desk, tilt his Trilby backward with a thumb, and inquire, "What's doin', Boss?" To my surprise, Mr. Saxon never seemed to take offense, possibly because his deliveryman's English accent had him buffaloed. In the fifties, Americans seemed in awe of anyone with an English accent, even my Derbyshire one, as though it indicated superiority in some way. I found this baffling, especially in a country where everyone was supposed to be equal.

It was Mr. Powers who, when he heard that Joe and I were planning a camping trip out West, warned me that under no circumstances were we to set up our tent near a highway. "There's guys drive them roads out there just lookin' for green-horns like you," he told me. "See, if you're camped by a road, they can make a quick getaway." This fellow had bought into the American scene with a vengeance and spoke in his version of a Mike Hammer accent. He still sounded English, although slightly demented.

My job with Rynex and Saxon included answering the phones, and putting together little packages of false teeth for Mr. Powers to deliver to dentists throughout the town. It was not an oner-ous task, and my salary was probably commensurate, although I don't remember how much it was; however it was enough to help with the groceries and eventually provided me with a pair of new shoes.

Around Christmas time that year, members of staff at the Geophysical Lab invited us to their homes, and I baked scones to present to our various hostesses. Our first celebration in the

United States was memorable for the fact that, having saved up for a bottle of barely affordable wine, when getting out of the car, Joe knocked it to the pavement where it shattered.

I had been with the company for almost three weeks when, one Sunday, Mr. Saxon and his wife, both of them probably in their seventies, invited us for a drive in the country. It was before we had accumulated enough money to buy a secondhand vehicle, and we happily accepted. The day of the excursion was dark and very cold for a Washington winter, and when the Saxons picked us up at our flat, Mr. Saxon tucked a rug about our knees in the back seat, and headed for the neighboring state of Maryland. It soon became clear what the blanket was for: Mrs. Saxon, her husband explained, had need of fresh air when they drove, so the back windows of the car had to be open. We cowered under the blanket and lied that it was quite all right. Mr. Saxon continued to drive slowly about the duller, flatter parts of Maryland, Joe and I becoming colder and more moribund by the minute, while outside the winter countryside rolled by in shades of brown or gray, the only bright color being the occasional flicker from a gas-station sign. There was no vestige of green anywhere, and I thought nostalgically of the brilliant green of Cromford Meadows at home where, as a schoolgirl, I had raced up and down the hockey field on cold, sunny winter afternoons. I remembered how it felt whenever I was able to smash my ball into the goal, the feeling of triumph when our school marked up another victory. I'd completely blanked out the more usual scene consisting of gray skies, rain, and mud.

CHAPTER 6

The "Gee Whiz"

AFTER I HAD WORKED at Rynex and Saxon for three months, a job became available at the Geophysical Lab, and at Joe's urging I went for an interview. The man in charge of personnel was an ex-admiral, and as I gathered later, we had not won the war because of him. He was certainly incompetent as personnel manager, especially in view of the fact that he hired me; I'll never be sure why he did, and wonder now if someone had hinted that Joe wasn't happy with his salary.

Before the Admiral interviewed me, I was taken into an office where Dolores, one of the Lab's two secretaries, placed me in front of a typewriter so that I could demonstrate my nonexistent prowess at the keyboard. I pecked out a few sentences, making several mistakes, was interviewed by the Admiral for five minutes, after which I learned to my astonishment that I had been hired as a receptionist "with some typing duties." The next day I handed in my notice to Mr. Saxon, who graciously congratulated me on what he saw as a step up, said good-bye to my fellow employees, and prepared to begin my new job the following week.

My position as receptionist at the Geophysical Laboratory of the Carnegie Institution of Washington—known to its employees as the Gee Whiz—was, I thought, unbelievably grand. I was stationed behind a huge desk in the middle of the main hall near the front entrance, where I was in charge of a typewriter, a telephone, and a system of bells with which to alert staff members when their guests arrived, or they were wanted on the phone. That first morning, men who worked in the shop and the research labs stopped by to wish me well. (There were few female scientists at the time.) One foolish man even brought me a paper to type. I began to feel, proudly, that I was contributing to important scientific work and, after having typed a few papers, found I was beginning to get a glimmer of what Joe was up to with his crystal structures, and what it was about the rocks that fascinated him when we drove through the countryside.

The Geophysics building with its sandstone facade consisted of two stories in Spanish style with a red-tiled roof. In summer its walls were smothered in yellow climbing roses, and Virginia creeper that in the fall turned bright red. There were many large shade trees near the building and extensive lawns that sloped gently downhill toward a long hedge of forsythia close to the road. Next door, a redbrick building housed a group of Catholic nuns. Both this and the lovely Geophysics building were razed a few years ago, and the Lab moved downtown to be closer to the other Carnegie Laboratories.

Joe's quarters at the Gee Whiz consisted of a small separate building next to the main one. It contained his office and some extremely primitive equipment, which was probably the reason members of the Lab called it "the Dog House." When we arrived, Joe, a neophyte x-ray crystallographer, first had to set about building his x-ray generator from scratch. Over several days, he gerrymandered the job using wire coat hangers, chicken wire, and an empty cocoa tin at a cost of two dollars. In keeping with the times, the computer equipment, also in the Dog House, took up a whole room.

The shop in the basement where lab equipment was designed was headed by Joe England, who oversaw the work of several men including a fellow named John Van den Huerk, a friendly but dubious type who on one occasion had a pair of woman's panties hanging from his rearview mirror. It was he who gave Joe his nickname: "Smitty." Before we had a car, Van often gave us a lift home after work. In addition to Dolores, the Lab also had a head secretary, Virginia Rappaport, who worked for the Admiral. There were also a couple of black janitors, Clarence and Joe, plus a gofer, a white man named Kirby from whom we later bought our first car, a two-seater.

On the first floor where I had my desk, there was a series of labs off the main hall for people who worked in various areas of geophysics. At the far end of the hall was Dr. Murray, an elderly geophysicist nearing retirement. Next to him Dr. J. Frank Schairer worked in two side-by-side labs between which he rushed, out of one door at a forty-five-degree angle and into the next, his pipe emitting sparks as he flew by. His research was mainly on the melting of rock-forming minerals, for which he used furnaces in his attempts to reproduce this phenomenon. Schairer was a friendly man, and energetic in all he did. He told us stories about his days helping to set up the Appalachian Trail, and his fraternizing with bootleggers who had their stills among those mountains. They made him welcome, and he spent time around their campfires, swigging their illegal booze. The trail had been initiated during Franklin Roosevelt's administration, in the hope it would help mitigate the widespread unemployment of the time.

Schairer had been at the Lab in the 1930s during Prohibition when Professor Cecil Edgar (C. E.) Tilley, Joe's professor from the Cavendish Lab back in Cambridge, came to the Gee Whiz for a sabbatical for six months in 1931 so that he and Frank could do some research together. Prohibition meant that no liquor was then available in the States, and the two of them often nipped up to Canada and back on weekends, returning with Schairer's car laden with illegal hooch. Tilley had been Joe's straight-laced boss at the Cavendish Lab, and he found it hard to swallow this tale until Frank assured him that after Tilley came to the Gee Whiz he became a changed man.

Schairer had an objectionable lab assistant, whose idea of a joke was to bring to the lab a huge inflated figure of a scantily clad, large-bosomed woman, and set it up in the doorway of the lab just behind where I sat at my desk. Schairer soon put paid to that, and the figure disappeared shortly thereafter. Frank was always occupied. He was busy running his furnaces for research even after his retirement in 1969; tragically, he died while swimming off the east coast of Maryland a year later.

Another scientist, Dr. E. G. Zies, a modest, elderly man, was an expert volcanologist who some years later, when we were back in Cambridge, visited us on his way home from a conference in order to fill Joe in on what he had learned about ancient Finnish volcanoes. Felix Chayes, a younger scientist, told us that the Depression had reduced him to selling apples on the street. Frank Tuttle, the man who recruited Joe for the Geophysical Lab, was famous among geophysicists for his study of the effect of high pressure on rock formation. Joe Gregg, a tall Canadian in his fifties, also worked at the Lab and became a particular friend.

I worked at the Gee Whiz from January 1952 until February 1954, and enjoyed myself greatly. The staff members were friendly, as I had found most Americans to be, and graciously accepting of my incompetence, at least to my face—what they muttered to each other behind my back, I never knew.

CHAPTER 7

Exploring My New World

AFTER WE HAD SETTLED in, Joe's colleagues began to invite us home: the Chayes, the Schairers, the Tuttles, and Dolores the secretary, who invited us to her parents' house where we saw our first television program, which of course was in black and white. Joe Gregg, the tall Canadian, was our most frequent host. I suspect he was looking for company since he was a bachelor living alone; we often got together with him at The Hotte Shoppe on Wisconsin Avenue for lunch or dinner, and sometimes he drove us out into the countryside, where I finally had to admit that the American landscape was not so bad, after all.

One of our longer trips was west through Virginia as far as the Blue Ridge Mountains, on the way passing through the Shenandoah Valley with its mile after mile of cherry and apple orchards. (This colorful valley has since disappeared under suburban housing.) It was spring when Joe Gregg first took us there and the fruit trees were in full bloom, while on the Blue Ridge blossoming redbud and dogwood trees added their delicate colors against the black outlines of trees not yet in leaf. It was also where we came across an example of coy Americana—a "comfort station"—a public lavatory.

After we had bought Kirby's old car, which had space for only the driver and one passenger, we did a lot of exploring on our own: Bull Run, Antietam and other Civil War battle sites, plus the narrow valleys of Virginia where farmers plowed with horses at hair-raising angles on the slopes. We often slept out at night, parked beside the road or in an old quarry, Joe stretched out in the front seat trying to avoid the gears while I slept along the back windowsill. We visited Jamestown, an early English colony, where at the time only the foundations of the houses remained—the town has since been reconstructed. Nearby was Colonial Williamsburg with buildings that dated from the end of seventeenth century and included the original Breton Parish Church, and rebuilt landmarks such as the Governor's Palace and the Raleigh Tavern. We found the town very handsome. It was the height of the tourist season, and the streets were crowded with visitors watching people dressed in eighteenth-century costume reenacting life in the early colony, using authentic speech patterns.

On the same trip, we traveled to Gettysburg where an actor playing Lincoln, in a sober suit and a tall black hat, intoned the Gettysburg Address. Later, we found a small stone armory at Harper's Ferry on the bank of Virginia's Shenandoah River where it flows between towering cliffs to meet the Potomac River. Just before the Civil War broke out, the abolitionist, John Brown, attacked the armory in the hope of providing weapons for his supporters before leading them south in a bid to end slavery. It turned out that supporters were few, and after his attack on Harper's Ferry, he was captured by Confederate General Robert E. Lee, tried, and sentenced to death.

One particularly golden day we drove to Jefferson's mansion, Monticello. It stands on a hill, and we parked at the foot and walked up to it through woods full of enchanting dogwood and redbud trees. A little below the house we came across a row of primitive stone buildings that had housed Jefferson's slaves. From the outside, I found the Palladian-style house heavy-looking; the inside, however was charming and livable, furnished as it had been in Jefferson's time, even to shelves full of books from the president's library. Jefferson and his family are buried in a garden near Monticello; the bodies of the slaves had been shoveled underground anonymously in an area away from the house. Jefferson also had a black mistress, Sally Hemings, with whom he had six children, another facet of American slavery of which I had not been aware. Many men, now regarded as heroes of the American Revolution, owned slaves, Washington among them. Often the unfortunate Africans were shipped from their homelands in English slave ships, a shameful legacy.

Jefferson was a practical man. He purchased an early letter-copying device called a "polygraph"; as the user wrote on one sheet of paper, another pen linked to it wrote the same words on another sheet. We also saw Jefferson's clock, which he had furnished with pulleys and weights; it was wound by hand and still told the correct time two hundred years later.

I learned more American history on these trips around the Capital and the countryside than I'd learned during the single term assigned to it at Ernest Bailey's Grammar School back home.

CHAPTER 8

The Back of the Bus and the "Red Scare"

IN WASHINGTON, AS THE summer blossomed, our northern blood began to find the region's hot, humid weather uncomfortable, then too hot, and finally unbearable. There was little domestic air conditioning then, and our apartment sweltered. We took showers, only to be soaked with sweat moments afterward; the only respite we found was in the movie houses. As a consequence, we saw a lot of films that summer, but I soon noticed that black people were nowhere to be seen.

During the fifties, particularly in Washington, DC, and the rest of the South, people of color were not allowed into "whites-only" cinemas, or to sit at "white" lunch counters. They also had to use bathrooms labeled "colored" (if any were provided; sometimes they were not). Black people also had to drink from segregated drinking fountains, often side by side with ones labeled "whites only." They even had to enter banks through a "colored" door, but once inside our bank in Washington, they could join a queue consisting of both blacks and whites.

On our first venture on a Washington bus, Joe and I sat toward the back. That had been my chosen position on my way to school during my Grammar School years, so that in

Washington I automatically went to the back of the bus. Later, when I told a friend we had traveled to the Lab by bus, his eyes took on a guarded look. "Where did you sit?" he asked. After I told him, he shook his head and told me of the local mores. This explained why we had been regarded with surprise by the conductor and the whites, while the black passengers had looked anywhere but at us. None of this had been shown in any American film I'd ever seen. And yes, there was racism in Britain although with a different, colonial flavor: people of color were seen, I'm ashamed to say, as "the white man's burden."

During my childhood, I never saw a black person because there were none living in our village or its environs. My first sight of black people was when American troops, sent to fight the Nazis during World War II, appeared on the streets of Derby. Afterward, there were a few children in the area with a white mother and a black father. My aunt Flo, a very traditional woman, surprised me one day after the war when I found her talking to a black girl on a street in her village. Fearful of her response to the stranger, I hurried over to them. She immediately introduced me and told me that the girl had to put up with "nasty comments" from students at her school. It was obvious that Aunt Flo was on her side.

In the 1954 Supreme Court ruling, *Brown v. Board of Education*, it was determined that school segregation was unconstitutional. As usual, different states all over the country had their own views on this. In the South, some were openly opposed, while others took as long as possible to comply. The law did not spell out how the ruling was to be accomplished, asking only that it be done with "deliberate speed." There had been a large influx of blacks from the South, which meant that most northern elementary schools were crowded, and both the teachers and the buildings stretched to bursting point. The more affluent whites moved their children into private schools, leaving black children and poorer whites in the crowded public schools.

In 1955, the position of black people in America began, very slightly, to change when Rosa Parks, a black seamstress from Montgomery, Alabama, bravely refused a bus driver's demand that she give up her seat to a white person. (Black people had objected to such demands before on Southern buses, so much so that drivers were now armed.) The next day, Martin Luther King Jr., then the minister of Dexter Avenue Baptist Church, helped organize a bus boycott, and since three-quarters of its riders were black, this almost put the Montgomery bus company out of business. Other local ministers of black churches encouraged parishioners to join the boycott, and most of them did. Many of them set up carpools to take their friends to church or around the city, and white women often had to drive their domestic servants to their job. A White Citizens' Council opposed the boycott, attacking people on the streets and setting fire to houses, Martin Luther King Jr.'s among them. The boycott lasted about a year, and in November 1955, the Supreme Court ruled that segregation on buses was unconstitutional, as was forcing black riders to pay at the front of the bus and enter through the rear doors.

During our early years on this side of the Atlantic, I began to learn a little about US politics. In England, I had been a Conservative, having been indoctrinated by my parents, and influenced by the fact that I had been a youngster in Churchill's wartime Britain. Nevertheless, it was not long after I came to predominantly right-wing America that I began my move to the left. I suspect that the beginning of this change came during the Red Scare, when any-one of a slightly leftist bent was assumed to be a Communist. The early 1950s was the time of the Cold War, when Russia and the West were at loggerheads. Senator Joseph McCarthy of Wisconsin denigrated innocent people, including Dr. Martin Luther King Jr. and many others, while J. Edgar Hoover, Director and founder of the FBI, used wiretaps, planted evidence, and harassed any-one who disagreed with his thinking. Some found their careers ruined by false accusations. Some of Hollywood's most influen-tial film directors, actors, and scriptwriters were accused of having Communist sympathies, including Lillian Hellman, Humphrey Bogart, and Katharine Hepburn.

One day, when I was on duty at my desk in the great hall of the Gee Whiz Lab, two men arrived, mackintoshed and trilby hatted, asking to see a member of the scientific staff. I was instantly alert. Lately, the FBI had been sending men, always in pairs, to interview anyone who had ever made an approving comment about Socialism, or the Soviet Union, or had a dreaded Red among his or her acquaintances. (At the time, Socialism and Communism were mistakenly thought of as synonymous.) It appeared that the American right to free speech was no longer sacrosanct. The men who showed up that day asked to see one of the scientists. I don't recall who it was, but I do remember my indignation as I reluctantly activated the bell to call the man they were seeking. Nothing came of this encounter, the scientist was not in jail the following day, but this was the height of Hoover's "Red Scare."

CHAPTER 9

First Trip West

HAVING WORKED AT THE Geophysical Lab for three months or so, by summer I had accumulated only a week's vacation; nevertheless, Joe and I planned a trip west. Our colleagues assured us that we would need at least three weeks to drive to the West Coast, because there was so much to see. Consequently, I bearded the Admiral, who at once agreed to my plea for extra leave. I've wondered since if perhaps everyone was happy to see the back of me, and my atrocious typing.

Generous colleagues lent us a tent, a small stove, and other equipment for our journey, after which we hit the road north. In the fifties, any trip to the Northwest meant taking the "Pennsy," the Pennsylvania Turnpike, a four-lane highway through the Appalachian Mountains. The road had been developed in 1940, the work supported by General Eisenhower, who later became president.

This was to be the only such super highway on our journey, in fact the only one then in existence. When I saw the turnpike for the first time, with traffic roaring down two lanes each way, I was relieved by the knowledge that, after this one, there were no more such highways lurking elsewhere. The first thing I noticed as we approached the president's famous road was a sign forbidding us to go above sixty-five or below forty-five miles per hour. I would have preferred an upper limit of forty-five miles per hour; nevertheless, Joe plunged bravely into the melee, I clutching the door handle as we joined the throng at a mad fifty miles per hour. (At greater speeds, our old car began to judder.) It was a couple of hours before I settled down and stopped hanging onto the door, and it was a relief to hit the Ohio border where the roads once again became civilized: one lane in each direction.

The weather was summertime hot, the car had no air conditioning, and we drove with our arms outside the open windows, each of us garnering a blistering sunburn on one shoulder—Joe's to the left, mine to the right. (I had not yet learned to drive.)

I don't know where we stopped in Ohio, but vividly remember Indiana because we camped at a park named Tippecanoe where my blood ran cold as we settled into the tent for sleep, and bears began crashing about outside. I have learned since that there were no bears in Indiana then; nevertheless, it took Joe a while to convince me that our lives were not in danger, and that the noise I heard was squirrels scampering among the trees. Apparently, in addition to being no Francis Drake, I was no Annie Oakley, either.

We headed first to Wisconsin to visit our friends Marilyn and Bill Bailey, whom we had met when Bill was doing a year's postdoc at Cambridge. At the time, his wife Marilyn had seemed to me the height of sophistication, although I was soon to discover that she was almost as much of a rube as I, never having been outside the United States or even the state of Wisconsin, until she visited England. On the way to Madison we passed through the environs of Chicago, but all I remember about the town during our first westward trip was a tram in a wide street. Later, we were to spend forty-five years in that city.

Madison was a quiet university town along the shores of four small lakes. Lake Mendota, the largest, is surrounded by low, wooded hills with, here and there, drumlins, little hills that give evidence of Wisconsin's glacial history. There are also moraines that loop across the state, formed when glacial lobes retreated, leaving behind their load of glacial till. Isolated blocks of ice made depressions, which, as the ice melted, filled the holes with water to form kettles. Glacial erratics, huge rocks dropped by the retreating glaciers, are scattered about much of the state. Often, they are nothing like the native rock, and could have traveled hundreds of miles from as far north as the Upper Peninsula of Michigan or Canada.

The Bailey's house, then on the edge of town, was adjacent to a farmer's field where a red barn housed a white horse that ran whickering to the fence whenever Bill's young son called its name. Bill was a geologist, and worked in Science Hall, a large red-brick building close to the Memorial Union. That first morning, we ate lunch on the Union Terrace overlooking Lake Mendota. The day was sunny and warm, the lake full of little boats, a few students swimming from the dock. After lunch we walked up a glacial drumlin topped by an observatory, appropriately named Observatory Hill. There, we enjoyed extended views of the lake and our first sight of Indian effigy mounds: one of a bird and the other a turtle.

After bidding farewell to Bill and Marilyn, we again headed west and found that the roads were not of the best, although people to whom we complained at a roadside diner where we stopped for lunch, assured us that Canadians often came south of the border onto US roads, looking for better traction for their wheels. We discovered the literal truth of this when later in our trip we crossed the border into Manitoba, and the tarmac turned abruptly into a dirt road that grabbed our tires and slewed us toward the opposite ditch.

After Wisconsin, our route took us to the port city of Duluth in northern Minnesota where, from a hill above the town, we could see iron ore being loaded into ships for the journey east and then south through Lakes Superior and Michigan, some of them heading for the steel mills of Gary, Indiana.

We had moved west, certainly, but still we seemed nowhere close to what I thought of as "The West." Flat Ohio hadn't done it for me, and Wisconsin had been comfortably like Derbyshire with its low green hills, cattle, and small farmsteads. Even with its fields of sweetcorn—not yet grown in England—its numerous advertisements for Wisconsin cheese, and its red German barns, it still felt like home.

The next night, we camped near Duluth, on the shore of Lake Superior, and the next morning attempted to take a walk through a nearby wood where we ran for our lives amid clouds of mosquitoes buzzing and swarming about our heads. Lake Itasca is officially the source of the Mississippi, which bisects the United States from north to south between Canada and the Gulf of Mexico, and runs over twenty-three hundred miles. A man camping nearby showed us a small spring near the campground, and its stream that flowed into the lake. He claimed that tiny flow of water as the source of the mighty torrent we were to cross later, on our way back to Washington, DC. In our early days at the Geophysical Lab, we visited that mighty waterway, and found it crowded with trawlers, and other sea-going boats bringing in goods from foreign parts. It made the River Derwent back home seem no bigger than a trickle.

Next came Manitoba in Canada, with its unpaved roads. We drove for many miles surrounded by huge stretches of wheat and corn, leaving clouds of dust behind us. We were headed for Winnipeg where Jane and Bob Ferguson had invited us to visit them. Bob was another of Joe's friends from the Cavendish Lab in Cambridge. We stayed two days with the Fergusons and their new baby, visiting the town and the university campus. Winnipeg was a handsome town, although my Derbyshire self found the flat countryside unappealing. Afterward, we drove south of the border again, headed for the Badlands of South Dakota.

Here was an area closer to The West of my imagination. As we drove, the land became more and more infertile until there were no crops or even rangeland in sight, only miles of dry, sand-colored, striated buttes where the crystallographer aboard, now in his element, insisted we stop to hack off a few rock samples to study back at the Lab. The sun was blistering, and the precipitous sides of the buttes, slippery with loose sand, showed no sign of vegetation.

Further west, in the Black Hills, we came across the old gold-rush town of Deadwood, another piece of the genuine West. There, we watched enactments of Wild Bill Hickok's and Calamity Jane's adventures, Joe as entranced as I. We stayed in town most of the day, wandering the streets where covered wagons creaked by, peopled by actors dressed in what we aficionados of the cinema recognized as western costume: the women in long dresses and bonnets, the men in heeled boots, jeans, bandanas, and wide-brimmed cowboy hats. We visited the cemetery at Boot Hill, where Wild Bill and Calamity Jane are buried side by side. Afterward we drove up to Mount Rushmore in the Black Hills to view the four famous carvings: Washington, Jefferson, Roosevelt, and Lincoln, and were dismayed to read that they had been carved so that tourists would have a reason to visit. For me, the hills were reason enough with their towering granite cliffs with their quartz and feldspar, their limestone caves like those we were familiar with in Derbyshire, their forests of pine and spruce.

The darkness of those trees above the dry, sand-colored Badlands had given them their Lakota name: *Paha Sapa,* or the Black Hills.

The Black Hills gold rush began in 1874 in territory deeded to Indian tribes, including the Sioux. Gold was found in several places in the area, most of it in Deadwood, at which point gold diggers from afar began to invade Sioux territory. In 1876, General George Custer led seven hundred troops to the area and was challenged by thousands of Indians, including the Sioux, the Lakota, and the Northern Cheyenne. The tribes routed Custer and his men at the Battle of the Bighorn, forever after known as Custer's Last Stand. Custer was killed in that battle. To the local tribes, the battle is known as the Battle of the Greasy Grass.

The granitic rocks of the area (not the ones with the Presidents' likenesses) came in for a pounding by Joe's hammer before we entered Wyoming, where we visited Bighorn Medicine Wheel Historic Landmark, which sits at an elevation of ten thousand feet in the Bighorn National Forest. It is a sacred site to various Indian tribes, including the Arapaho and the Crow. The Medicine Wheel consists of a huge circle of stones at the crest of a hill, with a small circle within it that has "spokes," also of stones, that run from the center to the outermost circle. Recent discoveries have led to the theory that the spokes indicate the position of the summer solstice, both at sunrise and sunset.

Our visit to the Wheel left us gasping, both because of its elevation above sea level, and the glory of distant view of mountains far to the west. It seemed we were well on the way to our target: the American West.

CHAPTER 10

Journey's End

WHEN WE REACHED NORTHERN Montana, I felt a surge of excitement. I had spotted mountains in the distance that had to be the Rockies, rearing up into the sky, gray and humped like a herd of slumbering elephants. Traffic was sparse and distances between settlements long, which made us realize why friends at the Lab had insisted we take cans of gasoline along with us, as well as extra food and water. We drove for two days through largely uninhabited prairie before we finally reached Glacier National Park and started looking around for somewhere to stay for the night. Even at the lower elevations, the night promised to be too cold for the thin sleeping bags lent by friends more used to camping in warmer, southern climates. We had little money, so that, when not staying with friends, we searched for campgrounds, or failing that, a cheap motel or B&B along the route. We had managed to keep to our rule that we would spend no more than four dollars a night; that night, the place we decided on after a long search cost us an eye-popping seven.

The accommodation was one of a group of cabins made of dark roughly planed wood, the inside walls smooth planks of pine. There were the usual small bedroom, bathroom and kitchen, and a wooden porch at the front where we ate our picnic dinner. The silence was deep, apart from the call of birds, and the whisper of wind through the pines that covered the nearby hills. After dinner, as we sat peacefully reading in the cabin's two worn easy chairs, someone knocked at our door. We looked at each other; we knew no one in this part of the country, and remembering the "bad guy" warnings given me by Mr. Powell at the tooth factory back in Washington, I was reluctant to open the door. Mr. P. had warned me that the roads of the United States are infested with dubious types out to rob rubes like us.

There was a second knock at the door, louder than the first, and when Joe opened it he found an Indian standing on the balcony wearing some sort of cloak over his jeans, moccasins on his feet, and a magnificent feathered headdress that framed his face. His arms were folded, his expression stern. This apparition raised one hand and pointed into the distance.

"Powwow," he said gravely. "Big teepee, eight o'clock."

Unfazed, Joe nodded. "Powwow," he said with equal solemnity. "Big teepee, eight o'clock. Thank you very much."

My husband was not easily disconcerted. Our visitor departed and Joe, closing the door, turned to find me dancing around the room, crying, "An Indian! An Indian!" (The term Native American had not yet entered the scene.)

I had met a couple of young men in Washington with no Indian blood in them, who claimed they earned money for tuition by dancing at tourist powwows; nevertheless, I felt certain that our magnificent chieftain could not have been a fake. I was ecstatic; it seemed we were "Out West" at last! We went to the powwow at eight o'clock as the Chief had instructed, but to my disappointment the man in the headdress did not appear. In fact, the occasion proved to be a gathering of what I feared could not be real Indians; their jeans and expensive sneakers didn't strike me as particularly authentic, nor did their stamping around in a circle and periodically grunting "Ugh." I wasn't sure what I'd hoped for, but this certainly wasn't it.

The next day, we left the campground by way of the Going-to-the-Sun Highway, a glorious road leading us up through the pines high into the Rockies. On one summit, Joe pulled into a picnic area at the side of the road, and we clambered out, hoping to catch a glimpse of the Pacific Ocean. We had traveled almost three thousand miles; surely the great sea must be on our door-step? But alas, it was not. To the north and south, to the east, and disappointingly to the west, were other mountain peaks, row on row, and evergreen forests continuing on as if forever. We learned later that these peaks and forests stretch three thousand miles north to south, and it became obvious that even the peak we were on would not be high enough to give us a glimpse of the Pacific. Time was getting short, and there were other places we'd been warned not to miss, such as Idaho, which has the largest stretch of lava in the country, and the famous Yellowstone National Park. The Pacific Ocean would have to wait for another time.

Driving southeast via Great Falls and Helena, Montana, we headed for the National Park's west entrance, which lay in the corner where Wyoming, Montana, and Idaho meet. There we found all kinds of natural phenomena that more than made up for our loss of the western sea. There were the animals: bighorn sheep, bison, and elk. We were happy not to run across grizzlies, or wolves, although we saw a great many brown bears, and many foolhardy visitors feeding them through their car windows. I was sorry not to spot a moose.

There were geological features round every bend in the road, and Joe informed me that the park lay over a hotspot deep in the earth's mantle. This heat caused a plume of magma to rise, erupting a total of three times as a supervolcano, the most recent 640,000 years ago, leaving a caldera (a volcanic crater) at least forty miles across. We visited the so-called paint pots of yellow-colored, sulfur-smelling mud that bubbled and writhed, and hot springs breathing out clouds of steam. When we returned to the park again in 1965, we found that an earthquake had destroyed them, leaving behind a small hilly area of yellow-colored sand; the mud pots were long gone. Rugged volcanic cliffs gleaming with black obsidian loomed above the waters of Yellowstone Lake.

In order to widen his knowledge of crystallography, Joe had also studied geology, and we often stopped to collect rock samples along the way. Joe's enthusiasm was contagious, and awoke in me a lifelong interest in rocks, so that today I can still identify some of the more common varieties: marble, sandstone, limestone, granite, quartz, obsidian, and other volcanic products.

We were thrilled to come across Old Faithful, a geyser so named because legend had it that it exploded at exactly one o'clock each day. Today we know that the geyser spouts every ninety minutes, more or less, depending on how much water it produced during the last episode. Other geysers, sometimes groups of them, produce taller plumes of water. The western scenery continued to be breathtaking, and at times even frightening for people raised in the softer countryside of England.

The park is roughly the size of Connecticut and there was much more to see, but we were able to enjoy it for only three days before we reluctantly packed our gear and began our long trek home to Washington.

When we were close to home, driving across a bridge that spanned the Rappahannock River in Virginia, the sudden jerking of the old car jarred me awake. We had been used to this "juddering" whenever we approached fifty miles an hour on the super highway, but the traffic was heavy and Joe had been driving slowly as we approached the bridge. When the car began literally to hop its way down the highway, it became obvious that something was seriously wrong, so we lurched toward the nearest gas station.

The mechanic's prognosis was not good: "You need new gears," he informed us. "It'll take at least a week." All of which meant that we had to leave the car at the station and travel back to the nation's capital by bus, dressed in shorts and hauling backpacks. That doesn't sound unusual today, when shorts and backpacks are *de rigueur*, but it was different in the 1950s, as we discovered when we walked through Washington's downtown streets where men on a construction site and youths in passing cars whistled and catcalled.

I was a young woman and used to yobbish types whistling when I passed construction of any sort—such men would whistle at a kilted Scotsman—but this time it became obvious that Joe was the object of their delight. Apparently it was forgivable if I wore shorts in town; it was not so for my poor husband. With relief, we caught a passing tram and hurried off to the sanctuary of our apartment.

CHAPTER 11

We Like Ike

ON JANUARY 20, 1953, one of Joe's fellow scientists invited us to visit the downtown office of a friend of his in order to watch President Eisenhower's inaugural parade along Pennsylvania Avenue. The office was five stories up, he told us, overlooked the route, and would afford a good vantage point. As two green-card immigrants, we had taken no part in the recent voting, but of course we accepted the invitation. Ike had been our hero ever since he and the forces under him—American, British, Colonial, and Free Europeans of every sort—had saved us from Hitler and his Nazis.

Seated on chairs at an open office window, we had a clear, if distant, panorama of the parade. The day was overcast and about forty degrees Fahrenheit; nevertheless, the president and his wife rode in an open car flanked by bodyguards—some on foot, some on motorbikes—waving to the crowd as they were driven slowly down the Avenue. Further along the route were grandstand seats, some reserved for members of the government and for military officers. Others, priced between three and fifteen dollars, were for hoi polloi.

Ike's long, white car was followed, after an interval, by regiments representing the army, navy, and air force, as well as various female regiments. Many civilian groups also marched, including officials from various states, accompanied by floats carrying townspeople dressed to represent their state's history or occupations and flanked by members of their police forces on motorbikes. There were sixty-five bands in the parade. No doubt they were playing a variety of patriotic tunes that we listeners in the clouds were too far away to be able to distinguish one from another, but we could see the strutting drum majors tossing their batons around their backs and over their heads to unbelievable heights. The march went on for some hours, while below us streamed rainbows of color from the different uniforms, and the twinkle of gold and silver from trumpets and drums. Over three hundred horses took part, as did an Alaskan dog team.

Below and around us, every window was filled with spectators, and cheering citizens crowding the sidewalks were held back from the parade route by rows of police. Later, it was estimated that at least one million people watched the parade. For us neophytes it was an amazing spectacle, the whole panorama brought to what we found an unbelievable finish by three elephants, symbols of the Republican Party.

The parade had been magnificent, but its solemnity, which for us had been eroded by the lumbering elephants, was further undermined when the driver of a small, yellow vehicle following close behind, hopped out every so often to shovel up steaming piles of dung to add to his load.

Little Smitty

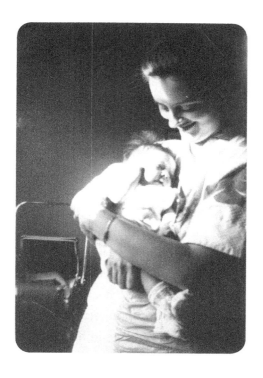

A LITTLE OVER A year later, in February 1954, our daughter Virginia Ann was born. I continued at work until then, through the early days of morning sickness and beyond. During the pregnancy, Joe and I spoke of our new family member as "Little Smitty," not because we particularly wanted a boy, but because

Clarence, one of the janitors at the Lab, assured me that I was expecting a son. I had noticed him observing me closely when I passed him on the stairs, until one day he told me he was watching me in order to make his prediction.

"You start up them stairs left foot first every time," he explained, "and that means you gonna have a boy."

Clarence was disappointed in me when Virginia arrived— maybe my being left-handed had skewed things—but he always made a fuss of her when I brought her to visit the Lab. Of course we thought the newcomer perfect, as do all new parents; we, however, were right. We had not produced a Smitty, but perhaps faute de mieux, Smithy became my pet name for Joe from then on. We named our first child Virginia after the state that borders Washington, DC, and in recognition of the fact that Virginia is the first member of Joe's and my families to be born in America.

I can't claim to have known a great deal about coping with a baby because my mother had her younger sister, Aunt Gladys, to help with my brothers and sister. Consequently, as a youngster I had little childcare thrust upon me, apart from wheeling my young brother Gib about the village in his pram. As a mother, I was a complete amateur. Fortunately, Ginnie was not a difficult baby, apart from her normal nighttime wails, so other than stumbling around groggily during the daytime, I didn't do too badly in my new role. In any case, I had only the early buildup toward a Washington summer to contend with before it was time to prepare for our journey home to Cambridge, more bearable climes, and some grandmotherly assistance. Joe's postdoc appointment at the Geophysical Lab had been for three years, and would be completed by June. He had been offered a job as a lecturer at the Cavendish Laboratory at Cambridge University.

We enjoyed our final spring in Washington, and at the beginning of June set off for New York. We were both happy to be going home. Joe was looking forward to taking up teaching and research at his alma mater, while I was ready for help with our new arrival. We boarded the *Queen Mary*, steerage class this time, but with a cabin of our own. Members of the crew were supportive and helped by warming up Virginia's baby food and getting rid of her disposable napkins, and after a long, tiring trip to Portsmouth by sea, to London and then north by rail, our train at last pulled into Derby station.

It was a happy reunion. My mother and father were there, as were Joe's parents, along with his sister Hilary. There was much hugging, coupled with ecstatic greetings for the newcomer from her grandparents, after which we set off for home in my father's car. The first thing I noticed as we drove out of Derby was how small everything looked: the houses, the roads, the cars; but Ballantrae, my parents' house, with its pantry in the space below the stairs, was just as I remembered it, and it was good to be home.

My mother had hauled out from somewhere the huge metal cot with sides that let down that had been my sister Beryl's haven, and had set it up in the sitting room, along with a bed for Joe and me. A week later, when we were settled, Joe left for Cambridge in order to find somewhere for us to live.

I had become pregnant again (I attribute this to the ambiance of the *Queen Mary*). "Oh, you naughty girl!" my mother-in-law said when I gave her the news, and I decided that either she thought this would be a virgin birth, or she was afraid her son's climb toward promotion at the Cavendish was about to be hampered by my fecundity. However it was, we welcomed a second perfect daughter, Susan Hilary, born in Cambridge in March 1955. My father drove my mother down from Derbyshire so that she could look after Virginia; she and Joe took turns visiting us at the hospital each day.

Childbirth in England and America proved to be very different. In England, natural childbirth was the norm: the mother produced her infant without anesthetics and was encouraged to yell as much as necessary. (I confess that in Susan's case it was a relief when it turned out that I would need to have a caesarean.) When Virginia was born in Washington, the practice was to give the mother an anesthetic that "allowed her to react," that is, yell her head off, but have no recollection of any suffering afterward.

The hospitals, too, were quite different. In America, I had a room to myself; in England, I occupied one of a series of beds lined up in a row in a ward. In America, I was sent home after two days; in England I was in hospital for two weeks because of the C-section. All mothers in England were given at least a week to recover from childbirth.

Autres temps, autres moeurs. Both methods produced two excellent daughters, and I am grateful. And so now, with two children in tow, I settled even further into my role as materfamilias.

CHAPTER 13

Cambridge: The Cavendish

AFTER FOUR MONTHS OF living with my parents, or on Joe's parents' farm, in September 1954 Joe took up his lectureship at the Cavendish Laboratory in Cambridge.

Built in 1874 and funded by William Cavendish, the seventh Duke of Devonshire, the Cavendish was the first laboratory in the United Kingdom devoted to experimental physics. It is widely considered the world's most famous physics laboratory, and has had a history of monumental breakthroughs. Its first head, James Clerk Maxwell, formulated the classical theory of electromagnetic radiation, which was the basis for the field of special relativity and quantum mechanics, and helped usher in the era of modern physics. Einstein described Maxwell's work as the "most profound and the most fruitful that physics has experienced since the time of Newton."

The succeeding Cavendish professor, John William Strutt, discovered argon, predicted the existence of surface waves, and described for the first time dynamic soaring by seabirds.

Cavendish professor Ernest Rutherford began the revolution in physics, which led to the discovery of quantum mechanics in the 1920s. One student, J. J. Thomson, discovered the electron; another, Charles Wilson, invented the cloud chamber, and a third, Ernest Rutherford, who went on to become Cavendish Professor, discovered artificial nuclear fission. James Chadwick discovered the neutron.

The Cavendish Laboratory played an important role during World War II, when much of the early research on radar and atomic physics was conducted there. When Germany invaded France in May 1940, British officials invited a small team of French physicists to continue their research on slow neutron capture at the Cavendish. Known simply as the Paris Group, physicists Frédéric Joliot-Curie, Hans von Halban, Lew Kowarski, and Francis Perrin were the first to propose that heavy water be used as a moderator for a nuclear reactor. In 1953, Francis Crick and James Watson made their monumental discovery of the double-helix structure of the DNA. Their lab was just down the hall from Joe's, when he arrived in 1954.

Most importantly for Joe, Cavendish professor Ernest Rutherford, who took over in 1938, developed the use of x-ray crystallography as an extraordinarily powerful tool for under-standing the structure of biological molecules. Joe had been deeply involved with x-rays at the Geophysical Laboratory in Washington, and while there had built his own x-ray generator from miscellaneous old equipment, chicken wire, and a cocoa tin at a cost of two dollars.

One of Joe's mentors at the Cavendish was Helen McGraw, the only women on the scientific staff and one of very few women in scientific work at the time. After gaining her BA and PhD from Girton College, Cambridge, she joined the Cavendish in 1946, where she remained for the rest of her scientific life. Like Joe, Helen became interested in the crystal structure of feldspars, which make up most of the surface of the earth and the moon. In 1989, Dr. Megaw became the first woman to be awarded the Roebling Medal of the Mineralogical Society of America. Probably due to her influence, throughout his life Joe was a strong advocate for women working in the sciences.

At the Cavendish, we became friends with Stuart Agrell and his wife Jean, Peter Gay, Mike and Hilary Bown, and Bill and Ingrid Cochrane. Bill was gruffly Scottish; Ingrid, fair, pretty, and Swedish. Mike and Hilary Bown remained at Clare College, Cambridge, and our family and theirs became lifelong friends. Mac MacKenzie and his wife Anne had by now left Washington to return to the University of Manchester, and we also saw them occasionally.

Joe found a place for us to live in a row of semidetached houses on Lovell Road off the route to Ely, to the east of the college. It was built of yellow brick and had two stories, with upstairs the usual two bedrooms, bathroom and box room, and downstairs a dining room, sitting room, kitchen, and glassed-in porch. There was also a long vegetable garden at the back where Joe was kept busy at weekends when he wasn't at the Lab.

We settled into domestic life, to which I was not yet fully accustomed. I had worked ever since I left Ernest Bailey's Secondary School at sixteen, first at the county library, then the Washington tooth factory, and finally the Geophysical Laboratory; consequently, I was not used to the routine or the loneliness of motherhood. I had, however, grown up in the thirties when women, if the family could afford it, took on housework and mothering after they married. Sometimes, less well-off women were hired to do the housework, or work as nannies, or babysitters. There were also jobs for women in shops, restaurants, and factories. The men, meanwhile, earned money for expenses or "twined it in," as the Derbyshire phrase had it. They were not expected to do anything else, aside from administering an occasional spanking when the offspring got out of hand. Joe was different from other husbands of the era, and often took care of the girls, either by having one or the other in the pram while he was gardening, or wheeling them out on walks, and to the local shops when food supplies ran low. My mother was taken aback by such unmanly behavior. "Your dad would never have done that!" she told me. "How does Joe find the time?" So-called househusbands were far in the future.

Joe's mother, father, sister Hilary, the girls, and me at Lovell Road.

And so our new life in Cambridge began, and I spent it cooking, cleaning, taking care of the children, visiting friends and having them visit me. I got to know several neighbor women with young children, so I was able to swap babysitting from time to time.

At weekends, after doing the week's grocery shopping, Joe and I often wheeled the girls in their pram near the Backs beside the River Cam, or over the paths through the fields to the nearby town where Rupert Brooke once rented a room, and later wrote his famous poem "The Old Vicarage, Grantchester" ("Stands the church clock at ten to three? / And is there honey still for tea?"). Brooke and several friends met in the town, these included Virginia Woolf (with whom he is reputed to have swum naked in the Cam), Bertrand Russell, and John Maynard Keynes. They were part of a group that met at the now-famous orchard and tea-room opposite the church in Grantchester. It was where we often called in for a cup of tea and a scone. In spring, when the weather was warm, we sat outside, luxuriating on deck chairs and enjoying the blossoming glory of the apple trees.

When term was over, we went home to Derbyshire for a month or two, staying sometimes at my in-laws' Birchwood Farm, where as a baby Ginnie slept in a well-padded wardrobe drawer in the sitting room. On other occasions, we stayed with my parents at Ballantrae House. Joe spent his time back on the farm doing work he loved: the chain harrowing, haymaking, harvesting, and the milking, clad in ancient tweed trousers and jacket, and the old black sweater his mother saved for such an occasion.

When I wasn't busy helping my mother-in-law in the kitchen and looking after the girls, I caught up with my Durward relatives in Matlock, and my Wallis grandmother. While I was in America for the first time, my beloved grandfather, John B. Wallis, died. He was a naturalist, writing a daily nature column in the *Sheffield Telegraph*, as well as an accomplished painter. I wrote about him extensively in my earlier memoir, *A Pennine Childhood*; my favorite painting of his graces the cover of the book. His death was a huge loss to me; it was he who taught me to love the natural world, and I loved visiting him and my grandmother Wallis at their home in Whatstandwell, overlooking the Derwent Valley and the canal, where we took many walks.

After his death, my Granny Wallis went to live further up Whatstandwell with her youngest daughter, Flo. All three of us carried the name of the famous nurse, Florence Nightingale, who grew up in the village of Holloway, just north of Whatstandwell. My grandmother was "Florence," my aunt was "Flo," and I am Brenda Florence. Granny Wallis lived to be ninety, and was still able to bend over to lay her palms on the floor well into her sixties, much to my juvenile envy.

In these early days, my brothers Pete and Gib, and my sister Beryl, were still living at home: Pete, then in his early twenties, was working at a local iron works; Beryl, after graduating from her Catholic secondary school, worked for an electric company in Belper, and Gib was still in school.

On this and subsequent visits to Derbyshire, in addition to calling on Smith and Wallis relatives, we enjoyed walking along the canal paths and other public footpaths in the area, meeting friends at various pubs, and attending events such as well dressings at local villages. We also drove further afield to visit University friends in London, Durham, Manchester, Edinburgh, and Glasgow. We had settled in well to our new life.

However, about two years later Frank Tuttle again loomed onto the scene. It was he who had recruited Joe for the Geophysical Lab in Washington; this time he represented Pennsylvania State University. He had come to offer Joe an assistant professorship at Penn State to which he had moved the year before. In Cambridge, Joe's chances of promotion and tenure were slim. Leaving Britain for jobs in other countries, as Joe had done for three years, meant that when a more senior position became available it was awarded to a stay-at-home.

There were several of these men in the department, which meant that Joe's hope of promotion was nil, and the Pennsylvania chance was too good to miss. We decided to take Frank's offer; Joe because he had to if he wanted to advance in his career; I with reluctance, feeling, in today's idiom, "Been there, done that."

And so, for the second time, we became members of the Brain Drain. I took the necessary deep breath, and we gathered ourselves together once more, gave Joe's brother Tom, who was about to be married, our furniture, some of which is still extant at Birchwood Farm, repacked our suitcases and faithful cabin trunk, said good-bye to our people, and headed for the Liverpool docks where the *Maasdam* of the Holland America line awaited us.

CHAPTER 14

Pleasant Gap, Pennsylvania

IT WAS NOVEMBER 1956 when we sailed out again into the turbulent Atlantic, this time with two children in tow. It was not long before enormous waves were towering over the deserted decks, and not only I, but most of the passengers and even some of the crew, began to toss up their breakfasts. Not that anyone was eating breakfast, or much else; the restaurants were deserted, as were the library and the bars. Joe, however, rose magnificently to the occasion. Ginnie, who was almost three, and Sue, almost two, were among those not too badly affected by the vigorous rocking of the ship, and their father valiantly ushered them into the nursery where, as the children crawled about and enjoyed the toys, he spent much of the day sliding back and forth on his behind as the nursery's wooden floor reared up, first one way and then the other, as the ship tackled the waves.

On subsequent days, when the sea was less violent and we were allowed on deck, the girls and I spent the time huddled together on a reclining chair under several blankets. The voyage took six days, during which enormous waves tossed the ship about as if it were made of cork. Eventually we were bruised as though we had suffered a round in the ring with a world-class boxer. It was a huge relief when the ship docked at Hoboken, New Jersey, across the Hudson River from Manhattan.

After we had been through Customs—I being careful this time not to mention any recent gifts—we took a taxi to the nearest small hotel, where the girls and I waited for Joe to find a used car. He was successful, and the next day we began our journey to Pennsylvania in an ancient Plymouth, a long, low vehicle that looked to me as big as a small bus. Because of its size, Joe was able to fasten the back seat onto the roof, and crowd our trunk, suitcases, and some x-ray equipment into the boot and the back of the car. The girls and I sat beside Joe on the sofa-like front seat. (In those days, we weren't aware of the danger of allowing children to sit beside the driver; moreover, seat belts and airbags had not yet appeared on the scene.)

We had not visited Pennsylvania before, except to pass through it on the turnpike on our way out West in 1952, and I was happy to find that much of it, particularly the countryside around State College, home of Penn State University, was green and wooded with many small lakes and rounded hills. The town had been built where two diagonal lines drawn on a map of the state intersected at the center. It was a quiet, isolated little town surrounded by farms. In the 1850s it had been the site of the Farmers' High School, which by 1859 had become an agricultural college. When we arrived in November 1957, it was the Penn State University under the presidency of Ike's brother, Milton Eisenhower. At the time, the university was famous for its Division of Earth Sciences, which it claimed was the best in the world.

The hospitable Tuttles welcomed us into their home, as they had when we moved to the Gee Whiz in 1951. We stayed with them until we found a furnished house to rent in a village about ten miles from the university.

Pleasant Gap had a tiny center consisting of a food store, the police and fire stations, and a few scattered houses, one of which was ours. Behind this cluster, a road with more houses along one side led steeply uphill. At the top was a post office surrounded by a forest of pines that was home to a herd of deer. There were many hunters in the village, and in deer season gunshots echoed on the wooded side of the road as we pedestrians, keeping our heads down, walked up the hill to retrieve our mail. (There was no postal delivery in Pleasant Gap.) During the year we lived in the village, at least three hunters were accidentally shot, one of them fatally.

Joe soon plunged into his teaching and lab work, exchanging rides into town each morning with a neighbor who was studying forestry—the university was still partly an agricultural school—and I continued in my role as materfamilias. I spent my time much as I had in England: looking after the girls, cleaning the house, washing clothes, and shopping for food. Every day I'd go to the store for a bag of cookies, most of which I ate myself, which gives some indication of how bored I was. For laundry, I had both a washer and dryer, fortunately, because hanging clothes outside in that state's icy winters would have produced uncomfortably frozen underwear.

The town's citizens were mostly working class. They tended to be friendly, but a little wary of people from the university. However, two neighbors were more at ease with me: one, an older woman who lived next door and, enchanted with the girls ("Gee, those accents!"), occasionally invited us to her house where we enjoyed coffee while the girls played with her grown children's toys. The forester's wife and I also visited one another now and then. These were the only two people I had to talk to apart from the children until Joe came home in the evening. Meanwhile, a teenaged girl, the daughter of a local plumber, asked if I needed a babysitter. At first, I was unsure if I could use her, not having anywhere to go or the means of doing so—I didn't drive, and there were no buses or trains in or out of Pleasant Gap—but after Joe offered to teach me to drive, the possibility arose of being able to take myself off to State College to visit friends. I tried out the girl one day while I visited the next-door neighbor, and found her competent and acceptable to the children. However, one evening we came home unexpectedly early to find the sitter almost *in flagrante* on the sofa with a thin, spotty youth from her high school. Shortly thereafter it became obvious that she was pregnant, and her mother, tardily locking the stable door, announced that her daughter would do no more babysitting. I felt guilty about the episode on our sofa, until a while later when I met the new grandmother outside the post office, almost incandescent with pride as she showed off her newly arrived, barely legitimate, grandson.

It was January when Joe taught me to drive, and an unusually snowy winter, but every Saturday for some weeks, with the girls in the back seat, he took me out for a lesson. "Don't let your husband teach you. It'll only lead to trouble," the forester's wife warned. It was true that Joe had swerved a time or two when he was thinking a little too deeply about his feldspars, but surely he wouldn't think of his work when teaching me to drive? It turned out that I was the source of the children's fear, and Ginnie and Sue cowered on the back seat while I, attempting to change gear, sent the vehicle hopping down the road like a kangaroo, or when I braked too quickly and flung them against the back of the front seats.

Apparently they felt even more afraid when we combined a driving lesson with a trip to the dump. There was no garbage collection in the village, and we were expected to take our bags of rubbish to the local dump, which was located in an old, abandoned, very deep quarry. While there, I would back toward the edge of the cliff that overlooked the quarry before Joe got out to retrieve the bags of garbage from the boot and toss them into the abyss. Watching this operation through the back window of the car, our daughters, terrified that they too were about to plunge over the cliff, were relieved when Joe told them to get out so they could see that the car was a safe distance from the edge.

After a while, I decided I was ready to take the driving test, which I passed with no trouble. I was a good driver, although "I sez it meself as shouldn't," as old Derbyshire people declare; moreover I maintain that learning to drive on Pennsylvania's snow-covered hills explains my prowess today.

CHAPTER 15

State College, Pennsylvania

AFTER A YEAR IN Pleasant Gap, Joe and I found a house in State
College, the home of Pennsylvania State University, where Joe
worked. It was on Hamilton Avenue, in a quiet neighborhood
with homes made of brick or wood with the usual boring open
lawn at the front. However, it also had a long, narrow back garden that contained a huge evergreen near the house, several apple
trees, two willow trees, and a vegetable plot. The apple trees made
me wonder if American children ever indulged in scrumping—
stealing fruit—as we used to do in Derbyshire.

The house had a living room, kitchen, and dining room on the first floor, and three bedrooms and a bathroom upstairs. There was also a large basement, half of which was a garage, the other half the site of an old, coal-fired furnace into which, like firemen on a train, we periodically shoveled coal. Frank Tuttle's mother lent us the money for the down payment.

Joe and I settled down into our respective niches: child and home care for me; teaching, research, and weekend gardening along with the occasional golf game for Joe. On the surface, life was much as it had been in Pleasant Gap, except that we were closer to friends from Joe's department: American, English, Canadian, and various graduate students who were our age or a little younger.

The Dallam family lived opposite our house on Hamilton Avenue. They had a big weeping willow tree in their garden, and the children would gather the branches in their arms and swing. Ann Dallam and her husband Bill, a teacher, had three children: Kimmie, Billy, and Franky. Kimmie was Ginnie's age, Billy was Susie's, so they had friends to play with nearby. On occasion, when Joe and I were going out for the evening, we would drop the girls off at the Dallams, where they played, and were already in their pajamas when we returned to collect them.

One day I took the girls to play with the Dallam children, and Ann informed me that they were getting over chicken pox. If children had the illness when they were young enough, it was believed that if they developed the pox later it would be a much milder case. Ann suggested that Ginnie and Sue be exposed to the germs. Sue remembers being told to give Billy a hug and a kiss. Despite this close contact, the illness was not passed on, and the girls would have to wait a few more years before succumbing to the pox.

We also visited other friends, most of whom had children. The Herzogs, Lisa and Len, owned a house in Boalsberg, a small town nearby, where the girls played with their eldest boy, Fritz, and his sister Heather. A third child, Clayton, was born in 1964.

Len was a geophysicist who worked with Joe at Penn State, where he pioneered geologic age determination based on radioactive decay. In 1961, he founded Nuclide Corporation, which designed and built mass spectrometers. These instruments were chosen by NASA to analyze moon rocks brought back by the Apollo 11 mission, for which Joe was the chief investigator.

State College was quiet. I remember no parks or children's play spaces within the town, although there was an amateur theater where the girls and the Dallam children saw *The Wizard of Oz*. There was also a movie house, but we had to drive to Bellefonte, a nearby town, for our library books. There were few cafés or restaurants, the most upmarket among them was at the only hotel, the Nittany Lion Inn. (Local wits called it The Nittany Lyin'-In.) The other cafés were small mom-and-pop places. Thankfully there were no McDonald's or other dispensers of unhealthy foods; Americans were much slimmer then.

When we lived in Pennsylvania, it was the age of green stamps, which we "earned" every time we bought groceries, petrol, or anything from a drug store. We were provided with small books in which to stick the stamps, and when we had enough, we drove to a town about forty miles away to cash them in for a saucepan or perhaps a half dozen wine glasses. What a nuisance they were! Had the town where we cashed them in been a little closer, the goods we chose might have been worth the trouble; on the other hand, if we didn't collect our "prizes," we children of the Great Depression and wartime rationing were overcome with guilt.

We often drove the girls to play in various beauty spots such as Whipple's Dam, a small lake in a nearby county park. There were several such lakes in the vicinity, most of them with picnic tables and a sandy shore, where for some reason the sand was too fine for the usual sand pies. However, the girls played there happily enough, catching salamanders and "swimming" in the warm, shallow water.

Almost every weekend we visited the university's cow barns on the edge of town, where we felt at home among the farmyard smells, good and bad; they brought back memories of Birchwood, my in-law's farm among the Derbyshire hills. When we first moved to State College, we found a kitten at the barns and were allowed to take her home. However, through living wild, she was not at all tame and frequently terrorized the girls by leaping, claws out, onto their backs. We returned her to the barn.

Sometime later, we found a cat nestled in a corner of the barn with a litter of kittens that had just been weaned. A young agricultural student who was working nearby suggested the girls choose one of the kittens to take home. I suspect that anyone working about the barns had been encouraged to help get rid of as many kittens as possible; the place was, to use another Derbyshire word, "snidered" with cats. There were four kittens in this particular group, and Susan picked one out while Ginnie chose its name: Stripey, from which you will guess its predominant pattern.

Meanwhile, I registered Virginia at a nursery school, where Miss Bissy—small, plump, and gray-haired—was the teacher. Both Virginia, and later Susan, loved Miss Bissy, but Mrs. Boyd, Ginnie's teacher in kindergarten, proved to be a martinet: when a boy used a mild expletive in class, she marched him to the bathroom and washed out his mouth with soap.

Having some free time after the girls went to school, I registered to take a course in wood sculpture, taught by a young woman who rented an empty shop front on Main Street as her studio. I enjoyed the hammer-and-chisel work and eventually produced Wooden Willy, a figure rather like those on Easter Island, which now graces, if that is the word, a corner of my dining room. He was my only production in the genre.

My father and mother, and Joe's mother.

In the late fifties, my parents visited us in State College, accompanied by Joe's mother; his father had to remain to milk the cows and take care of the farm, helped by his son Frank and daughter Hilary, who still lived at home.

In addition to taking them to the girls' favorite place, the cow barns, we also drove them down to Washington to show them the Capitol, Washington Monument, and where we had lived when we first arrived.

The girls were thrilled to have their grandparents visit, and pleased to receive three silver dollars, one from each grandparent. For myself, I was delighted to show them around State College, which they seemed to like.

I had come to love Penn State, but my scientist husband was getting restless, and I knew another change was in the wind.

CHAPTER 16

A Heck of a Town

IN 1960, ABOUT FOUR years after we moved to Pennsylvania, Joe was courted yet again, this time by Julian Goldsmith, Chairman of the Department of Geophysical Sciences at the University of Chicago, who offered him an associate professorship. Joe told Julian he'd be interested if he'd make that full professor. After some discussion, the university agreed, and Joe become the youngest professor at that time at the University of Chicago.

I again braced myself to move, this time northwestward. The U of C, one of America's major universities, was well known for its scientific departments, and would be an ideal place for Joe to continue his geophysical work.

Joe drove to Chicago to be interviewed, and when he returned we made our final decision. *Our* decision, you ask? Anyone who was born in the early part of the last century will be aware that the decision was almost entirely Joe's: he found the idea exciting because of the U of C's fame in the scientific world. Outwardly, I went along, although inwardly exasperated. I was sick of moving, and in any case wanted our next move to be back over the Atlantic.

However, like most of my class and generation, I had been raised with the expectation that the man made the living, while the woman, no matter how reluctantly, made it possible for him to do so. In any case, it seemed I had few skills acceptable to America that would allow me to give much support to the family, and Joe needed to advance both as a scientist and as a twiner-in (breadwinner). Almost as important, we had discovered that the pension at the Penn State University, which was paid for partly by local taxes, was not recoverable if one moved to another state. This was not true of the U of C's pension fund with TIAA-CREF. Like many other women then (and too often now), I had no real choice.

And so we again began the ritual of gathering ourselves together. I hauled out and packed the suitcases and the faithful cabin trunk, hired a moving company to deliver the furniture, Joe crammed what was left into the car, and after final and tearful farewells to the Dallam family, the Herzogs, and other friends, we set off for Chicago.

It was a long journey, the children subdued, not even quarreling or fighting to preserve their space in the back seat amid the odd bits of luggage that we hadn't found room for in the boot. To add to our gloom, when we were about half way to Chicago and had pulled into a rest stop to eat our sandwiches, we found that we had lost Stripey, our beloved cat from the State College cow barns. We thought she must have slipped out when one of us went to the bathroom. Consternation! Recrimination! Copious tears! We searched for her for almost an hour, the girls crying, Joe and I calling, all of us beating the nearby bushes. Eventually, Joe and I agreed that our pet was gone, and after many tearful demands that we stay and look "one more time," Joe reluctantly pulled the car onto the highway and, amid howls from the back seat, we again took the road to Chicago. Over an hour later Stripey miraculously reappeared, crawling out of a heating duct in front of the driver's seat, to be greeted with hugs and more tears.

At Gary, on the southern edge of Chicago, we passed the steel mills that were then roaring full blast, and drove into the city through some of the worst of Chicago's slums, where the poverty of its residents was manifest: tumbledown, smoke-blackened apartments, rusted cars parked along the streets, people huddled in inadequate clothing on the sidewalks. None of this endeared me to my new home, even before I found that two huge coal-burning chimneys at a power station to the south of campus were spewing out so much smoke and soot that the air was beige. As we drove into Hyde Park, the South Side neighborhood where the university is situated, the few stockyards that were still active to the west of town made their presence felt; in addition to being beige, the air smelled horribly of burning cow. To add to my disillusion, after the first snowfall that winter it turned out that Hyde Park snow was black.

Nevertheless, after we arrived on Chicago's South Side, I knew that it was time to make the best of it, time to unpack the car once more and begin our new lives in this, the fifth place Joe and I had called home since we were married nine years earlier.

CHAPTER 17

Chicago: The Second City

CHICAGO, WHICH BY 1960 was the second largest city in the United States, was like nothing I'd ever seen. When I was younger, I had of course gone to London from my home in the English country-side, including a visit with two of my aunts who worked as maids at

Buckingham Palace. But Chicago was nothing like the more sedate, historic London or even my first American city, Washington, DC, which now seemed fairly tame. From the fiery steel mills of Gary, to the desolate slums of the South Side, and the dynamic downtown seven miles north of our new neighborhood of Hyde Park, Chicago was a study in contrasts: great wealth, and abject poverty.

Once the home of Native Americans, whose name for wild leek, called *chicagoua*, gave Chicago its name, by the late sixteen hundreds this area was the territory of French explorers, missionaries, and fur traders. In 1812, the Potawatomi Indian tribe drove out US soldiers stationed at Fort Dearborn, and it wasn't until 1837 that Yankee businessmen invaded the area, beginning its transformation into a world agricultural, financial, and architectural powerhouse, and driving out the native Indian tribes.

Chicago was ideally located; on the edge of the vast American Plains, all railroads to the east and west led to Chicago. By the late eighteen hundreds, eighty percent of farms in the Corn Belt were within five miles of the railway, bringing grain and corn to the Chicago markets and hogs and cattle to the city's slaughterhouses. From the Civil War, which tore the nation apart from 1860 to 1865, until the 1920s, and peaking in 1924, more meat was processed in Chicago than any other place in the world.

In 1914, the poet Carl Sandburg wrote of Chicago:

Hog Butcher for the World,
Tool Maker, Stacker of Wheat,
Player with Railroads and the Nation's Freight Handler;

CHICAGO: THE SECOND CITY

Stormy, husky, brawling,
City of the Big Shoulders:

They tell me you are wicked and I believe them, for I
have seen your painted women under the gas lamps
luring the farm boys.
And they tell me you are crooked and I answer: Yes, it
is true I have seen the gunman kill and go free to
kill again.
And they tell me you are brutal and my reply is: On the
faces of women and children I have seen the marks
of wanton hunger.
And having answered so I turn once more to those who
sneer at this my city, and I give them back the sneer
and say to them:
Come and show me another city with lifted head singing
so proud to be alive and coarse and strong and cunning.
Flinging magnetic curses amid the toil of piling job on
job, here is a tall bold slugger set vivid against the
little soft cities;
Fierce as a dog with tongue lapping for action, cunning
as a savage pitted against the wilderness,
    Bareheaded,
    Shoveling,
    Wrecking,
    Planning,
    Building, breaking, rebuilding,

Under the smoke, dust all over his mouth, laughing with
white teeth,
Under the terrible burden of destiny laughing as a young
man laughs,
Laughing even as an ignorant fighter laughs who has
never lost a battle,
Bragging and laughing that under his wrist is the pulse.
and under his ribs the heart of the people,
    Laughing!
Laughing the stormy, husky, brawling laughter of
Youth, half-naked, sweating, proud to be Hog
Butcher, Tool Maker, Stacker of Wheat, Player with
Railroads and Freight Handler to the Nation.

Because this "City of the Big Shoulders" was situated on the western edge of Lake Michigan, the second most western of the Great Lakes, it also became a huge port, with steel produced in Gary, Indiana, just south of Chicago, shipped throughout the world. Its relative proximity to the Mississippi River meant that Chicago controlled access from the Great Lakes to the Mississippi River basin. As the largest city near the vast grazing areas of the Great Plains, Chicago could indeed become "Hog Butcher to the World."

The Great Chicago Fire of 1871 destroyed the center of Chicago, but soon the city was rebuilt, and the small frontier outpost swelled, first from influxes of European immigrants, Germans, Irish, and Scandinavians in the latter part of the eighteen hundreds, and then starting in the 1890s, Jews, Czechs, Italians, and Poles.

With the onset of World War I, European immigration tapered off, while demand for manufactured goods increased. To meet the need for new workers, representatives from northern companies traveled south to recruit black workers, many of whom were only too glad to flee the Jim Crow South with its discrimination, lynching, and violence. This was the beginning of the Great Migration, which lasted until 1970. In all, six million blacks left the South, and traveled north and west, many of them to Chicago, where most of the men found work in factories or as porters on the railways, the women often as domestics.

African Americans from the South brought with them their jazz and blues, probably the greatest cultural influence on this midwestern city. By 1970, there were one million African Americans in Chicago, representing one-third of the population, most of whom lived on the South Side.

Chicago was a booming town, as well as a study of contrasts and, as I was soon to discover, I was not in the slightest bit prepared for it.

CHAPTER 18

The University of Chicago and the Columbian Exposition

Courtesy, The University of Chicago.

THE UNIVERSITY OF CHICAGO, one of the foremost universities in the United States and a research powerhouse, was an impressive place, with its magnificent neo-Gothic buildings, shady quadrangles, and scads of Nobel Prize laureates.

Almost all the university buildings and its faculty was situated north of the "Midway Plaisance," a several-mile-long, three-block-wide boulevard of grass and elm trees that stretched between Garfield Park to the west and Lake Michigan to the east, created in 1893 for the Chicago World's Fair, also known as the

Columbian Exposition, which celebrated the four hundredth anniversary of the arrival of Columbus in the New World in 1492.

The Exposition itself covered more than six hundred acres, and featured nearly two hundred new buildings (some meant to be temporary) of predominantly neoclassical architecture. Over twenty-seven million people from around the world attended the Exposition during its six-month run.

The Midway Plaisance had been built with areas sunk below road level to act as lagoons for boating, leaving on either side a grassy space to accommodate the fair with its entertainment: A Ferris wheel; shows such as hootchie-kootchie dancers, kiosks where goods from China to Dar es Salaam were sold. Dvorak himself conducted classical music, and Scottish, Welsh, African, and Hawaiian bands played their national tunes.

There were serious lectures, too, often given in halls especially built for the purpose. Some of those buildings were still in use when we arrived, and continue to be today: one in Hyde Park close to Lake Michigan had become the Museum of Science and Industry; another building that had been the downtown quarters of the Exposition's management now housed the world-famous Art Institute of Chicago.

The Exposition's symbol, a statue called the Golden Lady, graced an intersection behind the Science Museum.

When we arrived, the lagoons were long gone and had been grassed over, leaving Hyde Parkers with a pleasant walk under elm trees and, in the winter, a sunken skating rink. This stretched east as far as Wooded Island with its serene Japanese garden designed by famed American landscaper Frederick Law Olmsted, and the Lakefront, with its magnificent views of the downtown skyscrapers and, on a clear day, the Indiana shore. (Olmsted, who also designed New York City's Central Park, found his inspiration in Joseph Paxton, an English landscape architect who designed the gardens at Chatsworth House in Derbyshire, not far from where I grew up.) Mounted police, whose horses were stabled at the west end of the Midway, patrolled the area.

As newcomers, we were provided by the University of Chicago with an apartment at Faculty Housing—a yellow brick building on Ingleside Avenue just south of the Midway. It was on the edge of the neighborhood of Woodlawn, which, at that time, was referred to as a "ghetto" or "slum," and was almost entirely inhabited by black people who lived in poverty due to the discrimination they faced in education, housing, and employment. Woodlawn was dangerous for anyone, white or black, so we never went for walks south of our building, although Sixty-Third Street was a bustling street with easy access to Chicago's elevated railroad, the "El," from which you could travel all over the city.

As he had at the Gee Whiz Lab in Washington, Joe continued his work as "an entrepreneur in the development of instruments," as his colleague at the U of C, Professor Robert Clayton, later called him. Joe's first job at Chicago was to build an electron microprobe for the Department of Geophysical Sciences, and to develop techniques to make it work. Another of Joe's colleagues, Professor Peter Wyllie, wrote, "In the early 1960s, there were many analysts who said that the electron probe would never yield quality results because there were just too many problems. The task was rather like making science fiction become fact. The Chicago department was one of the first to have a successful instrument, an instrument that is now ubiquitous in geology departments. Twenty years later, Joe devoted similar efforts to the ion microprobe."

Joe continued his work with his study of x-ray crystallography and geology. At the time, x-rays were still used without much thought: in shoe stores to gauge foot size; by dentists, often without the use of lead aprons either for themselves or their patients. One student told Joe that he'd x-rayed his genitals so that his girlfriend wouldn't become pregnant. It would be some years before common sense broke in and practitioners of crystallography became more aware of the danger of x-rays. There was a theory at the time that, if one or both of the parents worked with x-rays, they would produce girls but no boys. We had Ginnie and Sue; I'm not sure that proved the theory, but there seemed to be an abundance of all-girl families among the scientists who worked with x-rays, though Joe would probably say that it was too small a sample to be statistically significant.

When we first arrived in Chicago, Julian Goldsmith, who was responsible for Joe joining the U of C, and his wife, Ethel, welcomed us with a dinner at their house in order to introduce us to other members of the department, among them Martha Clayton, a psychologist, and the wife of one of Joe's colleagues, who was to become a particular friend, and who lived on our staircase at Faculty Housing.

Martha came home from work in the midafternoon, and after I had picked up the girls from school, I would often put a teapot and cup on the staircase as an invitation to join me for tea. Also on our staircase was Saul Bellow, the famous author of novels, many of which were based on Chicago, and who occupied the top floor with one of his five—consecutive—wives.

With Martha Clayton, Lisa Herzog, and her daughter Heather, outside the Museum of Science and Industry.

Ethel Goldsmith also became a friend who later introduced me to campus life, the various women's clubs, and to the women who worked as volunteers at the U of Chicago Bobs Roberts Children's Hospital, where I was soon pushing a library cart around the wards and reading to the children. Not exactly the librarianship I'd practiced in Derbyshire, but more interesting to me than household chores.

CHAPTER 19

Lab Scabs

BESIDES MAKING THE POSITION of full professor as a condition of his employment, Joe insisted that our daughters attend the University of Chicago's Laboratory Schools. It was a private school, owned by the university, where almost all of the U of C faculty children were educated. The only other option for our daughters was a school in the Woodlawn ghetto, which would be far too dangerous.

In order to be accepted by the Lab School, students had to take an IQ test administered by the School, and it was said that in order to be accepted, students must have an IQ over 128 points. Joe and I had no idea how our girls would have scored, because when we showed up, Joe insisted that they be admitted, IQ test or no IQ test. The university must have wanted Joe sufficiently because they waived this requirement. As far as we know, our daughters were the only children at Lab School at that time to have been admitted purely on a parent's say-so.

In 1960, the tuition at the Lab School was a whopping $1,000 per year; with Joe on the faculty at U of C, we only paid half, but it still seemed a prince's ransom.

The Lab School campus was lovely. It covered two full city blocks, one containing the school building—neo-Gothic like the university, complete with turrets and ivy—with a lovely court-yard. The modern high school had been built at one end of the courtyard, leaving a large grassy expanse with trees, paths, and a small sunken amphitheater lined with benches that led into the high-school cafeteria. It was here that the students performed Shakespeare for the Renaissance Fair each May. Scammons Garden, to the north of the school, was the site of class picnics, vegetable plots, and the annual Easter egg hunt. Across from the school, on the second city block, were Sunny Gym, a playground, tennis courts, and Jackman Field with its baseball diamond and track.

The school was founded in 1894 by the education reformer John Dewey. Rejecting the notion that children should sit quietly and learn by rote, Dewey claimed that children learn best when they are busy doing something. A proponent of experiential learning, Dewey and his theories were at the heart of the Lab School's philosophy. And so along with learning to read, write, and do math, students put on plays, planted gardens, learned to square dance, and watched eggs hatch in a nest with a real hen.

The School was relatively small with around eighty students per grade. The children knew everyone in their own grade, and many others as well. As they moved up through the school, they could visit old teachers, and in the case of art, language, music and gym, often had the same teacher many times throughout their school years. This produced a feeling of continuity, and a warm sense of community. Students could begin their schooling in kindergarten, and stay under the same extended roof all the way through high school. In the fall of 1960, Sue started kindergarten, while Ginnie, who already had a year of school under her belt from State College, was enrolled in first grade.

Every morning, from our home in Faculty Apartments, Joe took Ginnie and Susan by the hand and walked them across the Midway, before going to his office in Rosenwald Hall, a limestone building in the main quadrangle. There were other children in Faculty Apartments, all going to Lab, so the parents set up a "carpool," or in Joe's case, a "walkpool."

All the other parents drove the four or five children the half mile to the Lab School, and dropped them at the front door. Joe, however, as an Englishman and a farmer's boy, insisted on walking, leading the children across the Midway and east to their school. Ginnie has said that she dreaded the weeks that Joe was in charge; the other children saw no possible reason for walking when they could be driven, and when Joe was out of sight, complained mightily. When it was very bad weather even Joe agreed to drive. The only problem was that he insisted that all occupants of the car wear seatbelts, something few people did in 1960. Hence, more complaints from the children. Joe, in so many ways, was a man ahead of his time, but it sometimes made things a little difficult for his children.

The early grades were fun for the girls, and teachers created a warm sense of belonging. Their classes often went on field trips, walking to the Oriental Institute, the Museum of Science and Industry, and Wooded Island, or taking the train downtown to the Field Museum, the Art Institute, or the Planetarium. In sixth grade the kids all went to Camp Farr, in Indiana, for a week of sleeping in bunk beds, swinging on a rope swing called the Big Dipper across a small stream, eating hotdogs and drinking "bug juice." The girls were vegetarians, and I had to send along cheese for them to eat in place of the meat dishes.

Language instruction began in fourth grade, and both girls took French all the way through senior high; starting so young was a great benefit. The physical education program was exceptional: along with the usual fare of softball, basketball, track and field, and soccer, the girls took swimming, gymnastics, ballroom dance, field hockey, fencing, tennis, and yoga.

There was a PTO—Parent-Teacher Organization—but it didn't have a deal of power. We were summoned to talks, during which the teachers explained to us what they were up to, but no one asked our opinion of the curriculum. Dewey's influence was evident at all levels of the school. In sixth grade, instead of reading about early human culture, students were given the opportunity to experience daily life in a fictitious Paleolithic community called Zinch Valley. There was much chipping and filing, and accumulation of dust, as the project dragged on and on. Each girl, in turn, did her stint in Zinch Valley, and by the end we all felt that this time Dewey's philosophy had been taken a bit too far. I teased them by asking if they were learning anything from their expensive education!

Another idea that floated about the school, although perhaps not an official doctrine, was that it was more important to understand the process than to get the answer right. This was all well and good, but I couldn't imagine it going over very well at my old school in Fritchley: "But, Miss, I know I got my sums wrong, but I know how to do 'um." Sue remembers one teacher saying that it wasn't necessary to memorize a lot of facts; you just needed to know where to look them up.

"Labbies" or "Lab Scabs," as they were called, often said they felt like guinea pigs, (although I suspect this was secretly a badge of honor). From time to time, students from the U of C would appear at the door of a classroom. Some would enter and sit at the back of the room, taking notes. Others, after speaking quietly to the teacher, would lead a child, or a small group of children to another classroom to be interviewed or tested, often under the guise of play. This kind of attention could make a child feel special, or else like a specimen under a microscope.

Despite all this experimentation, or perhaps because of it, most students received an excellent education at Lab. Notable alumni include Supreme Court Justice John Paul Stevens; Garrick Utley, a reporter for NBC; Valerie Jarrett, Senior Adviser to President Barack Obama; Arne Duncan, former US. Secretary of Education; Linda Johnson Rice, CEO of Ebony Media; Kennette Benedict, Executive Director and Publisher of the *Bulletin of the Atomic Scientists*, keepers of the doomsday clock; Sherry Lansing, former CEO of Paramount Studios; Lucy Kaplansky, folk singer and songwriter; and Malia and Sasha Obama, whose time at Lab was cut short when their family moved to the White House. The Lab School produced more doctors, professors, lawyers, politicians, scientists, artists, musicians, and writers than you could shake a stick at. It was a special place, with a great education provided. The girls did well, and on the whole enjoyed their years at Lab.

CHAPTER 20

Dorchester Avenue

IN 1962, TWO YEARS after we moved to Chicago, we decided to buy a house in the Hyde Park Co-op Homes, a new housing development about a mile from the University of Chicago. Consisting of attached, light-colored brick two-story townhouses built in a square, it was billed as a "cooperative housing development," in which the owners of the individual townhouses took turns serving as president, vice president, and voting members of the cooperative association, attended monthly meetings, and allocated money for the upkeep of the Co-op's roof and other areas shared by the residents. Joe and I each had a stint as president, and our duties included climbing up onto the flat roofs to investigate leaks.

The Co-op stretched between Dorchester and Blackstone Avenues, which ran north-south, and 55th Street and 54th Place, which ran east-west. There was a parking lot on the south end and an open space and playground in the middle of the square, called "the Central Area" or, more often, "the Middle."

Our house was the largest we had lived in since our marriage. On the corner of Dorchester and 54th Place, it had a kitchen/dining room, sitting room, and bathroom on the first floor, three bedrooms and a second bathroom on the second, and a basement. For the first time, each girl had her own room. Outside, there was a walled garden, and beyond the wall an area of grass, surrounded by a low hedge and three sycamores. Joe and I later added a birch tree and a lilac bush to the lawn, and installed a patio with flower beds in the walled garden.

While the house was being built, on weekends we often walked from our apartment in Faculty Housing on the Midway just south of the university to check how the work was coming along, the girls running among the builders' discards oblivious to danger—until Sue stepped on an exposed nail and had to be hauled off to the University of Chicago Hospital for a tetanus shot.

At that time, cooperatives were unusual, and reeked of socialism to most of America. Except for the inside of one's unit, a small front yard, and a small backyard, everything else was shared and had to be "in compliance" with the "Rules of the Co-op." The front lawns had to be grassed over—you couldn't, say, have a little vegetable garden—the trees could only be London plane trees (though as I said, we slipped in a birch in our more expansive corner lot), and there had to be a hedge between grass and sidewalk. Woe betide anyone who didn't cut their hedge to the required height! One couple on the southwest corner were both artists, and liked a Bohemian look to their hedge. After many entreaties, including Joe offering to cut their hedge for them, it was finally trimmed by edict of the Managing Board.

The ownership of the Co-op Homes was relatively diverse; there were a few university families, but most were not. Most children went to Ray School, the local public school, and then Kenwood High School, and not the Lab School and then University High, like Ginnie and Sue. In our Co-op there were white families, black families, a mixed-race family, and Asian families. Ginnie remembers being in the basement of a house belonging to a Japanese family and seeing the father, clad only in underpants, hurriedly pull on trousers; apparently, it was common in Japanese culture at that time for the father of the house to wander around in his underwear if only his own family was around.

Part of the responsibilities of belonging to the Co-op were the communal activities, such as potluck dinner, in which everyone brought food to share. Here, the men of the Co-op, muscles rippling beneath their T-shirts, cleared away dirt and rubble to

The men of the Coop digging a sandbox for the children.

create a sandbox for the children in the "Middle." Ginnie and Susan spent a lot of their time in the sandbox, and also playing "Cops and Robbers" on their bicycles, riding on the sidewalks around the houses, and dashing through the four openings that brought them and their playmates from the street into the Central Area.

CHAPTER 21

The DOGSheet and Other Pleasures

With Julian and Ethel Goldsmith.

THE DEPARTMENT OF GEOPHYSICAL Sciences was a close-knit, friendly group, led by Julian Goldsmith, who recruited Joe to the U of C. It had a department newspaper titled the *Dirty Old Gossip Sheet of the DOGS* (Department of Geophysical Sciences), or "DOGSheet" for short (the pun on dog poop is intended), launched and edited by Al Duba, a graduate student who later also did research on feldspars. The paper included much humor, news of student activities, and quotes from members of the faculty. Among those attributed to Joe were such gems as: "Pregnancy among grad student wives is highly contagious." "But that [being over thirty-five] doesn't stop me." "Actually, you *can* fool the feldspar!" "In my educational experience anything the students weren't enthusiastic about was what they needed!" And, "We were the ones running with the hot moon!"(See the later chapter on Joe's work on the moon rocks for a fuller explanation!)

One morning, after becoming engrossed in a research project that required his working on the weekend for many weeks, he said, "The hell with it, Brenda, it's Saturday; volleyball is more important!" After this he hauled the whole family off to join the departmental picnic in the Indiana Dunes, where volleyball was the main activity.

Among our most enjoyable times were the parties that we gave for students and faculty at our home. The first was in our apartment across the Midway, at which we met the "young Elders" for the first time: Wilf, a geologist, was a "Geordie" from County Durham in Northern England, and Lola, his wife, an Aussie from Adelaide, South Australia; both became close friends.

After we had bought the house on Dorchester Avenue, we continued to host parties for faculty and graduate students, where the street would echo with the shouts of professors and students riding our children's bikes or bouncing along on Ginnie's pogo stick.

The Dirty Old Gossip Sheet of the DOGS   Vol 1, No 12
"All the News that Fits!"   12-11-67

CHRISTMAS PARTY

The Dames of Geophysical Sciences (DOGS), the Chamberlin Rossby Society, and Prof and Mrs J V Smith invite all DOGS and friends to a Christmas party at 5455 S Dorchester on Friday, Dec 15. The party will consist of 2 parts--a carol and cookie session upstairs beginning at 7:30 to which participants are invited to bring their favorite Christmas goodies and concoctions for mass sampling and a "bring your own poison" affair which will begin in the basement around 9:00.

POETRY CONTEST WINNERS

The Chthonian Pundit III (T Weaver) won first prize in the first annual Howard B Zar Poetry Contest. Second prize(a lock of W Taffe's beard) was awarded to L F McGoldrick, who has the honor of collecting same. The winning entries are printed below, along with the entry of H. Zar.

FIRST PRIZE
I think that if I should find afar
A rock as lovely as H. Zar
A rock with such a granulation
To remind one of a railroad station--
Jumbled, confused, and a bit bizarre,
After all, it reminds me of H. Zar.
I think that I should throw it away,
Before people begin to stare and say:
"This kid's mind is in a fog,
Is it because he's only a DOG?"

SECOND PRIZE
e^x du/dx,
e^x dx,
sinh-1,
π
$\int r^2 dr$
Blows the mind of H. B. Zar.
(ED NOTE: π =3.14159)

NEW DOGSHOUSE
Gee, oh fiz ikil sigh
explain yourself, do try.
The minds of Hinds *(lousy typing)*
will XXX be've all kinds
'quaint idea, but why?

Is it that you're microprobic,
and it makes you somewhat phobic
to stand in the lines
behind greater minds
as they render your ear-lobic?
     H. B. ZAR

ED NOTE: Such a talent deserves
to have a poetry contest named
for him!

QUOTE OF THE WEEK
H. ZAR: "So you're the Chthonian
Pundit, You son of a....(ED-DOG?)

A RISING STAR?

I Lambert and J Robertson were featured in a smashing rendition of "Bombs Away" on Thur and Fri in Wb 5. Critics were amazed at the well-oiled performances and are convinced that I Lambert is indeed a star of merit and not just a "flash in the pan" as some described him following his magnificent performance in "Hellzapoppin!" with D. Mohr.

STORK RACE

Rumor has it that J. Albright has spotted A. Duba 7 days in a maternity race. Bookies are giving 7 to 4 odds on Albright, feeling that experience will out.

ZIEGLER ENTERPRISE NOTES

The Committee of Concerned Dogs has announced the formation of a new DOGS organization: the Society for the Defense of Fred Ziegler(SDFZ) IN French: Sous-Dogues pour Freddie Ziegler. Its motto is "Liberté, Fraternité, Ecologie." Crus Stashun, DOGSHEET reporter, says the society is a reaction to the adverse publicity received by Ziegler during the recent KKK-ENTRAILS-Artificial Indiana Limestone controversy.

NEW CONTEST?

MPOWB I has proposed a new contest for the Chamberlin Rossby Society next quarter: DOGSCRABBLE. Details will be forthcoming in a later issue of the DOGSheet.

Merry Christmas   *Happy New Year*

With the girls, I skated, not very well, under the stands on the U of C campus where research into splitting the atom had been carried out through the Manhattan Project, and also on the Midway, where a sunken area was flooded with water to make a rink.

In the late 1950s, Joe's brother Tom, and his wife, Glennis, moved from Derbyshire to Toronto, Canada, where he used his skills to become a building inspector. With Tom & co. only a seven- or eight-hour drive away, Christmas became more of a family occasion, with Tom visiting us at Dorchester Avenue with his wife, Glennis, and their twins, Henry and Alison, born in 1960. The twins were about six years younger than our two, but close enough in age to be companions during the visit.

Every year we attended Thanksgiving and Christmas Eve services at the University of Chicago's Rockefeller Chapel. The chapel, built between 1925 and 1928 and funded by the oil baron Nelson Rockefeller, was large enough to accommodate seventeen hundred people; its tower the tallest structure on campus. In addition to weekly Christian services there were concerts and lectures, and, more recently, services for people of other beliefs.

At Christmas, there was always a children's pageant at Rockefeller Chapel. One year, to general amusement, a young English boy, playing Joseph, knocked imperiously at the door of the inn and demanded, "Inn keepah! Inn keepah! Open the do-ah!" One of the highlights of the pageant was when Mary rode down the aisle on the back of an actual donkey. From the balcony of the chapel, Romy Wyllie, the wife of one of Joe's colleagues, acting the part of the Angel Gabriel, raised her arms and blessed the throng.

It was good to have family with us; the girls enjoyed getting to know their uncle, aunt, and twin cousins. One year, we drove up to visit them in Toronto for the holiday, a long journey through snow and numbing cold. Chicago's winters were severe too, but Canada's were worse, and we were glad when Tom and family decided that, in the future, they would rather come to us in the sunny south.

In Chicago, Joe and I resumed our Washington venture into classical music. I was still a neophyte at the time, my favorite music being jazz and the music of the Big Bands. The BBC's Palm Court Orchestra and its repertoire was the extent of my knowledge of classical music. Joe was a little more musically inclined than I, but not by much. Nevertheless, as the years went by we found ourselves looking forward to the glorious sounds we encountered every Thursday evening at Orchestra Hall in downtown Chicago. During the summer, the orchestra played outdoors at Ravinia, north of the city, and we attended a number of times.

Orchestra Hall, designed by Daniel Burnham, the man responsible for planning a great many of Chicago's parks, is a handsome building of redbrick with a light-colored stone trim. Its first-floor windows face the Art Institute across Michigan Avenue in Chicago's Loop. Over the years the orchestra has been conducted by several different maestros, among them Carlo Mario Giuliani and Sir Georg Solti. The former's approach to the music was gentle, even sentimental, the latter brisk, no-nonsense. I was happy with either.

Sometime in the sixties, knowledgeable people began to complain that the hall's acoustics dulled the sound of the orchestra; we who were not musicians were mystified: it sounded fine to us. That year, a large revamping of the hall was undertaken: one ceiling was lowered and reshaped. After this another group of aficionados declared that the acoustics were now even worse, and insisted that microphones be suspended here and there. I don't know what the state of play is today.

Joe and I both loved blues and jazz and listened to them often before moving to the United States, and of course while we were here. We thrilled to Benny Goodman's "Sing, Sing, Sing," Ray Charles's "Hit the Road, Jack," Nat King Cole's "L-O-V-E," Muddy Water's "Hoochie Coochie Man," Howlin' Wolf's "Smokestack Lightning," Ella Fitzgerald's "Summertime," and of course Louis Armstrong's "La Vie en Rose," "What a Wonderful World," "Moon River," "Little Walter," and "My Babe."

Chicago, and particularly the South Side, where we lived, was justly famous as the home of Chicago blues. Blues had originated in the Mississippi Delta area of the United States and had then traveled to Chicago after World War II with African Americans, who were searching for more freedom than they were allowed in the South. A large number settled on the South Side, making it the second largest black-occupied region in the country, next to Harlem, in New York.

The Delta blues, consisting primarily of voice, harmonica and acoustic guitar, was supplemented in Chicago with electric guitar, drums, piano, harmonica played directly into a microphone, amplified bass guitar, as well as occasionally a saxophone. Joe and I went to clubs on the edge of Hyde Park to hear bluesmen such as Muddy Waters, Howlin' Wolf, Buddy Guy, Paul Butterfield, and Charlie Musselwhite—a wonderful experience for us. We often found ourselves among the few whites in the clubs, but were never bothered, just as we were never bothered when we walked through the ghetto in Washington, DC. All of us, black and white, were there for the music, and what nights we had there, in the blues clubs on the South Side of Chicago!

CHAPTER 22

The Summers: Home to England

Punting on the Cam in Cambridge, England.

FOR ME, THE BEST part of Joe being a professor meant that he was on holiday during the summers. Of course, Joe was never really on holiday, and kept working on his science throughout the year, but it meant that we could spend the summers with our families in England. We were lucky in that the University of Chicago had a very extensive summer break, with the result

119

that we would dash onto a plane at Chicago's O'Hare Airport in early June of each year, and not arrive back until the third week of September. It was grand to be home!

Of course, as our lives changed in America, the lives of our English families changed, too. In 1953, Joe's father surprised us with the news that, now in his mid-fifties, he had bought a farm, his first. Ever since Joe was a baby, his mother and father rented Barn Close Farm in Fritchley, the village bordering Crich, where they raised Joe, his brother Tom, who was eighteen months younger, and Frank, three years younger than Tom. Joe's sister, Hilary, came along twelve years after Joe.

My father-in-law, Henry Smith, had created a neat, productive farm at Barn Close where Joe grew up, with a herd of dairy cows, pigs, and hens, and pastures of grass, grain, kale, and other crops. I knew they grew turnips, because Joe used to talk about eating them raw in the fields when he was hungry during the war when there was rationing. But Joe's father had always had a passion for owning his own farm, and as the second youngest of twelve children, ten of whom survived to adulthood, by the time the inheritance was given out, there was nothing left for him so he had to make his own way.

Birchwood Farm, on Longway Bank, near the village of Whatstandwell, was just on the far side of the Derwent Valley and several miles from Barn Close, where Joe was raised. It was part of the estate owned by Sir Richard Arkwright, Founder of the Industrial Revolution. It was originally advertised with about sixty acres, and a farmhouse dating to the sixteen hundreds. But

Henry Smith's Birchwood Farm.

before the auction, two parcels of land with stone buildings bordering the farm and running up to Cromford Moor were added.

After a year simultaneously running Barn Close and the newly purchased Birchwood, Joe's parents moved in on March 25, 1954, Lady Day.

Some years before the Smiths bought Birchwood, it had been a refuge for a local murderer named Smedley, who lived in Matlock on a street that ran parallel to that of my Durward relatives. Smedley murdered his young girlfriend at her home, fled, and spent some time in Birchwood's middle barns about a quarter of a mile up the lane from the farmhouse. He kept himself fed by stealing turnips from the fields and, as Joe's brother Frank told my daughter Ginnie, he made himself useful to the current farmer so he wasn't turned in to the authorities.

Smedley was later captured, spent many years in prison, and was released toward the end of the nineteen-nineties. An aunt of mine, who lived in Matlock, declared that the unfortunate murder victim had "asked for it." Such was the thinking of many people of the time; appallingly, to them the man was often blameless.

When Joe's father bought Birchwood, a young couple had been running it and lived in the house, which had electricity and a telephone, but no bathroom, just an outside loo in the wash-house. The land was not in good order, but was cultivated.

The purchase of Birchwood Farm led to a family split when Uncle Joe, Henry's older brother who rented, and later bought, Cross Farm in Crich, referred to Birchwood as "a bloody wilderness." Henry and Joe ceased speaking after that point.

However, wilderness or not, it was not long before my father-in-law made sure it was a wilderness that bloomed, and turned it into a real working farm. He brought from Barn Close his own young cattle, home-bred and tuberculin-tested, and bought and transported from Scotland a new batch of Ayrshire milking cows. He also had pigs, a bull, and a flock of sheep.

In addition to the meadows reserved for grazing, he and Frank, his youngest son, planted fields of wheat, barley, and oats, as well as vegetables such as potatoes and turnips. Joe's young sister Hilary helped with the sheep, and spent many a night with birthing ewes. After she left school, she worked at Lea Mills, the local hosiery company, in the design and sampling department. They did spin and manufacture cotton, but mostly wool. Granddad hired "a lad" to help him and Frank with the farm work.

Joe's brother Tom, a carpenter, builder, and general all-round handyman, worked on renovating the farmhouse, while Joe's mother designed the garden and added a flock of Rhode Island Red hens to the croft behind the barn and later the loft in the barn. Up the lane was what was referred to as the "camp field," where since the 1930s, families built small huts in which they spent weekends and summer holidays. Their rents gave the farm an additional financial boost.

Virginia and Susan loved their summers at Birchwood, and were soon helping their grandfather pick stones from the ploughed land, weed fields of potatoes, feed the calves, and milk the cows. They also enjoyed feeding the hens and gathering eggs with their grandmother.

I helped in the house, while Joe spent time doing the work he loved best after x-rays: driving the tractor during haymaking or harvest. As a very young man, he had decided that, if he failed to pass the Latin entrance exam, which was obligatory then if he wanted to get into Cambridge, he'd stay home, work for his father, and one day take over the farm. However, in six weeks, Joe managed to teach himself enough Latin to pass the entrance exam so he didn't take up

Grandad Smith, Ginnie, Susan, and calves.

a life working the land. But he felt such a continuing connection to farming that when introducing himself in his later years, he invariably told any new acquaintance that he was "a farmer's boy."

In 1962, Joe's sister Hilary married Ian Wellby, with my girls serving as the bridesmaids. Starting in 1969, Hilary, Ian, and Ian's parents ran an old people's home at Overton Hall, near Ashover. Overton had once belonged to Sir Joseph Banks, who from 1768 to 1771, during his long career as a naturalist, voyaged with Captain Cook to South America, Australia, and New Zealand. He introduced many new plants and trees to Britain, some of which can still be found in the gardens at Overton Hall.

In the fall of 1963, Joe's parents left Birchwood Farm in care of their youngest son Frank and his wife Nora. They had a young son, David, who was followed two years later by their daughter, Julie. Joe's parents moved to a bungalow in a nearby village. Joe's father spent six or seven years helping Frank on the farm, and then started going to Overton Hall to spend the mornings working in the kitchen garden.

My mother and father left our house in Fritchley that Dad had built, and where I lived from age eight until I left for America with Joe when I was twenty-three. They settled in a small house above Whatstandwell with beautiful views across the Derwent Valley, but it was only a few years later than my father died, leaving my mother a widow at only fifty-six.

My brother Pete was working as a commercial traveler, and was married to Pearl, a woman he met in the town of Newton Stewart where our Scottish relations lived. He had two sons, Stuart and Kevin, who were younger than my two.

My sister, Beryl, worked as a draughtswoman for a company in Milford, called GlowWorm, which made electrical fires and other appliances. From an extremely pretty little girl with fair curls and huge green eyes, my sister had grown into a very beautiful young woman, and soon attracted the attentions of Derek Taylor, an engineer and businessman, whom she married. Their children, Helen, Alison, Malcolm, and Andrew, were all younger than my daughters, but we spent quite a lot of time together.

My youngest brother, Gilbert, whom we called "Gib," was working in greengrocer's shops, and traveling down to Covent Garden in London to stock up on fruits and vegetables. He had a young wife, June, and two sons, Stephen and Ian.

We all continued to look forward to our yearly trips over the Atlantic, visiting relatives and renewing our acquaintance with favorite walks: the farm lanes, the local hills, the woods, and the canal with its coots and swans.

When the girls were still young, we sometimes spent a week or so in the summers traveling about Europe. One such trip was to Rennes in France to visit my old friend Ginette Thomas and her husband, Georges. Ginette and I had become pen pals when we were in secondary school just after the war. On this visit, Georges was retiring from the army, and we stood at the edge of the Rennes parade ground to watch a company of French soldiers, resplendent in uniform and medals, marching solemnly up and down, halting, saluting Georges and the other retiring officers, before marching off again. The men looked as soldierly as American troops, but remarkably small in comparison.

Georges drove us to the same chateaux my friend Margaret and I had visited on our maiden voyage to France shortly after the war. On the way, Georges pointed out a roadside memorial to his father and others of the French Resistance who had been part of the Underground that fought the Nazis. He told us that at one point his father and his comrades were captured. As they were being driven to a prison camp in the back of a truck, they overcame their captors and escaped, some into the fields, the others, including Georges's father, by diving into a nearby forest. Only those who chose the forest survived; the others were recaptured and shot.

During a later trip to Europe in 1969, we began our adventures in Paris, then traveled to Alsace-Lorraine, notable by Joe sampling perhaps a little bit too much of the high-quality wine and then singing in the street as we made our way back to the hotel. In Munich, I was horrified to come across a group of young men in a city park, their arms raised amid shouts of "Heil Hitler." The men were very young, and perhaps merely fooling about, but this was only twenty years after the war, and I was chilled. Later, I felt better when we drove south through the beautiful Rhine valley with its numerous castles perched on cliffs above the river that thundered below. I comforted myself with the thought that Germany has had a more benign history since the war.

By the sixties, the England I remembered from my childhood had changed a great deal. Apparently so had I. As a member of "the Swinging Sixties," my musical tastes now included the Beatles, Joni Mitchell, and the Rolling Stones, in addition to my growing love for classical music and the Chicago Symphony. By now, Bing Crosby sounded old fashioned to me, and I'd never liked Sinatra. (How can you like someone who had friends in the Mafia?)

Even my choice of clothing had changed: I now wore trousers, which had been verboten for women and girls in my village when I was growing up. I seem to remember I wore bellbottoms. My blouses were finished with a ribbon that tied at the neck, and I wore what were called wedgies: shoes with no gap between heel and sole. I didn't wear miniskirts, but welcomed the advent of a second choice, the maxi, which I wore with a fashionable, wide-shouldered blazer. I also indulged in a "mood ring": its "gemstone" was supposed to change color according to one's mood. Also fashionable were vivid colors and patterns from all over the world, along with belted cardigans, khaki trousers, and hot pants. I had definitely changed.

As I described in *A Pennine Childhood,* when I came across our old postman, I had to remind him of who I was. The last time I'd seen him I was twenty-three.

"I don't suppose you remember me, Jackie. I'm Brenda Wallis from Fritchley," I told him, at which Jackie's jaw dropped.

"Eeh, I say!" he exclaimed. "You 'ave altered!"

CHAPTER 23

Sweet (and Not So Sweet) Home Chicago

A photograph taken by Joe near the University during "urban renewal." His colleague, Professor Bob Clayton, is pictured.

AFTER OUR SUMMER IDYLLS with our family in the English countryside, we returned to Chicago, with Joe looking forward to going back to his work and Susan settling in quickly at school and with her friends. Ginnie and I, however, still longed for family and England.

But still, we were now Chicagoans. Joe and I ended up living in that city longer than we have lived anywhere else, longer even than our twenty-three youthful years in Derbyshire. We moved to Illinois in 1960 and lived there until we left in 2005, a period of forty-five years. As Dickens has it, those years contained periods, as do most lives, between "the spring of hope" and "the winter of despair." Fortunately for us, the bad times were interspersed with periods of everyday family life and yearly trips to Britain, Europe, and various parts of America.

One of the nicknames for Chicago was "Sweet Home Chicago," and indeed, some of our experiences were sweet— the excitement of living at a world-class university, the music, other cultural events, our friends, and the parties—but some of the day-to-day living was not. Hyde Park was not a safe area, and we were warned never to walk alone at night. There were gangs in the nearby ghetto of Woodlawn that sometimes invaded Hyde Park, although fortunately for us they were more concerned with fighting each other. The Blackstone Rangers and the Disciples fought many a battle, making life harsh and difficult for ordinary Woodlawn residents who only wanted to live their lives in peace.

The South Side of Chicago was then, and continues to be, a dangerous place. In the 1950s, crime had become so prevalent that the administration of the University of Chicago had discussed plans to pull up stakes and relocate the university, abandoning its gorgeous neo-Gothic buildings, to the much safer Chicago suburbs, or perhaps even Colorado.

Finally, the decision was made to remain in Hyde Park, and fight for a stable, mixed-race, mixed-income community by reducing what was referred to as "white flight," which saw white people fleeing to the Chicago suburbs. The university embarked on a plan of urban renewal and eminent domain, leveling tenements in Woodlawn, the neighborhood just south of it, and using the land for new buildings such as the University of Chicago Law School and mixed-income housing to stabilize the neighborhood. Of course, this had the shameful result that some of the poorest residents of Hyde Park and the contiguous Woodlawn were thrown out of their homes, which were then demolished.

But on the other hand, it also meant that the University of Chicago was able to remain in Chicago and add to the life on the South Side. Elijah Muhammad, the leader of the Black Muslims, called Hyde Park his home, as did Cassius Clay, later known as Muhammed Ali, as well as dozens of Nobel Prize laureates at the U of C. In the 1960s, Hyde Park was one of only several communities in the United States that was truly integrated, half black, half white, and stood as a sterling example of racial harmony in an extremely tumultuous time. The photo that Joe took in 1962 is typical of Hyde Park at the time; in the distance is the red-brick student dormitory, Pierce Hall, now demolished. Otherwise, the nearby area, only six or so blocks from the U of C Quadrangle, was urban blight.

However, in about 1965, things in the area began to change somewhat when the beleaguered citizens of the ghetto banded together to form The Woodlawn Organization in an attempt to rein in the local gangs and teach them that there were alternatives to fighting, raping, and shooting one another and their unfortunate neighbors. Training schools were set up to which both gang members, and youths who had managed to avoid being recruited by them, were invited.

Despite these attempts, the area was still plagued with murders and general mayhem: Shots were fired at our house, leaving three holes in Ginnie's bedroom window. When she came home from school the next afternoon, I had already moved her bed away from the window. A schoolmate of Virginia's was shot by a gang member; our house was burgled six times, mostly while we were away on holiday in England.

One intruder went so far as to search behind the books on Ginnie's bookcase and in Sue's desk drawer, where he found the silver dollars that their grandparents had given them when they had visited us in State College ten years earlier. Another time, our television was stolen. We called the police and were told that they had our TV. On our next call to ask when they would return it, we were told that they'd never had it in the first place. (Nothing much changes in Chicago's police force). Fights between the Blackstone Rangers and the Disciples left bodies strewn about Hyde Park, three of them in the warming hut at the 57th Street train station, where we used to shelter when we waited for an Illinois Central train to take us downtown, two in front of the 53rd Street YMCA.

No, Hyde Park was not safe. This hit us with a vengeance one night in November 1963, when Joe came home at ten o'clock one night with a black eye, having been mugged on his way home from the Lab. True to form, he tried to make little of the attack, at least to me, and told the girls and my mother who was staying with us that he had accidentally walked into a door. He later told me he had run after his attackers with the help of Abner J. Mikva, our US Congressman. Upon hearing Joe's cry for help, Congressman Mikva ran out of his house to help rescue Joe and chase the attackers. I was thankful Joe and his savior had been outrun, but mostly thankful for Congressman Mikva's courage in coming to Joe's rescue.

After that, Julian Goldsmith encouraged Joe to buy a gun, and they went to a store somewhere out of town where they both armed themselves with a pistol. Foolishly, we kept the weapon at the back of a shelf in the bedroom cupboard. Later, after we had bought a house in the country, Joe came to his senses and decided that owning a gun was madness. He buried it deep in the dune behind the house.

CHAPTER 24

Once More Out West

IN MARCH 1965, WE hit the road again, this time headed for California, where Joe had been invited as a visiting professor to Caltech, the California Institute of Technology, in Los Angeles. This meant that thirteen years after our aborted attempt to catch sight of the Pacific Ocean, Joe and I, now accompanied by our children, were once more on our way to the West Coast. This journey took us southwest through country we had not visited before, including our first stops at the Lake of the Ozarks State Park, and the George Washington Carver National Monument in Missouri.

The Carver National Monument was opened by President Franklin Roosevelt in 1943, the first national park dedicated to a black man. Carver, a farmer and owner of a small property, was educated, with a degree in the natural sciences. After graduation, he returned to his rural life with the intention of encouraging black farmers to be more productive, and switch from growing cotton, which both depleted the soil and encouraged the boll weevil, to planting peanuts, which enriched the soil and also made good fodder for both pigs and cattle. At first, mostly poor people ate the peanuts, which were boiled and offered for sale in outdoor markets. Later, they became popular with the more afflu-ent, either as nuts or as peanut butter.

In Oklahoma, the gentle hills were filled with coneflowers in bloom, and we saw the remnants of a trail left by the wagons of the earliest European settlers in the eighteen hundreds. As we moved west, the country gradually became drier and scrubbier, with tumbleweeds rolling across the land among nodding oil derricks. Among all this commercial dross, I spotted two meadowlarks, their yellow breasts brilliant against the brown landscape.

The Texas Panhandle with its high, flat tableland where oil derricks nodded to the horizon, was where we found lodging for the night in Amarillo, "a shapeless town," according to my notes. Further west, the land became flatter. This was the beginning of cattle and sagebrush country, with soil drifting in clouds below the wind. It was March and still very cold.

Soon, snow-covered mountains began to loom in the distance and we headed for Santa Fe, New Mexico, a town at an altitude of seven thousand feet. At first, the city seemed to me rather gloomy and squalid; however, I later found the center charming after we visited the historic Governor's Palace National Landmark. Historians have conflicting ideas about when the palace was built: 1610 and 1618 both have their defenders. (This was about the time the Puritans were colonizing Jamestown in Virginia and Plimoth Plantation in Massachusetts.) The architect of the Governor's Palace is unknown, but the adobe structure was to house Pedro de Peralta, governor of what was then Spanish territory. The palace and the San Miguel Mission in Santa Fe are the two oldest buildings in the United States. The town also has an excellent Indian museum, and in the plaza with its many quaint shops, I was amused to find an adobe Sears and Roebuck—very different from the building back home on the South Side's Stony Island Boulevard.

After Santa Fe, we entered mesa country. That afternoon we drove northwest to Bandolier National Monument where we climbed hills covered with juniper on their lower slopes, pines higher up. Later, down in the canyon where the cacti and pines were larger than any we had yet seen, we visited the tribal cliff dwellings that had been hacked out of the volcanic tuff. From here, we drove to Los Alamos, where the atomic bomb was tested with the help of former Nazi scientists, among them Wernher von Braun. Tom Lehrer, a comedian from the 1960s would sing, "'Vonce zee rockets are up, who cares vere zey come down? That's not my department,' says Wernher von Braun."

I found the town beautifully situated but dull. There, Joe visited fellow scientists at the National Lab, some of whom also worked in Geoscience, while the girls and I strolled the town. We returned to Santa Fe for the night, enjoying on the way a magnificent pink sunset that faded into a black sky crowded with millions of stars.

The next day there was snow and it was very cold. We visited Albuquerque to enjoy its quaint plaza, where we bought rugs, and afterward continued on through snow and hail to an Indian reservation in the driest, stoniest country we had yet come across.

That night, we stayed at a motel in the Indian capital, about which I noted, "of all the squalid messes, Gallup takes the cake." Forgive my youthful scorn; the motel was comfortable and warm, but I was beginning to think the glorious countryside far outstripped what its inhabitants, Indian or white, had produced.

The next morning, we left Gallup "at a gallop," and drove to Flagstaff surrounded by lovely, snow-covered hills, where I found the town to be "another grim mess in a glorious setting." It was then we approached our first real desert where there was very little vegetation, with Navajo hogans here and there, a few cattle, and soaring sandstone cliffs. The next day was bright and cold and we set off on the road that led to the Grand Canyon. The mile-deep cleft where the Colorado River roared beneath breathtaking cliffs was impossible to grasp on first acquaintance: too big, too glorious, and at the time, too cold and windy. We took a swift look and decided to return later. It was in Arizona that we first became acquainted with roadrunners: little, long-tailed birds with black crests, that ran along the sides of the highway. I later read that they can run up to twenty miles per hour, and are actually able to fly, but only do so to flutter up into a tree or to escape predators.

Because of the cold, we took a more southerly route to L.A. and drove first to Prescott, Arizona, a tidy little town set among granite hills. The houses and shopping areas were attractive, although, like many other places in the West, it was plastered with billboards. Again, the sunset behind the hills was a wash of red fading to pink over the snow-crested hills.

When we left Prescott, it was the end of March, the weather was becoming warmer, and on the other side of the mountains we found the desert in full bloom. There were several varieties of flowering cacti, including large yucca and barrel cacti. The floor of the desert and the mountain slopes were orange with California poppies, while white and yellow daisies, and blue lupines nodded along the roadsides.

At the California border, after having our car frisked for Colorado beetles, the border guards—no doubt hired by the fruit industry—queried us about any foreign oranges on board that we might be sneaking in. I had thought that some amendment guaranteed citizens the right to carry concealed oranges; apparently, I was mistaken. After we pleaded not guilty, we were allowed to proceed over the state border, where, amid the glorious perfume of orange blossom, we stopped and bought quantities of the local produce.

After this oasis, we were soon in the real California desert: no vegetation whatsoever, and a stretch of bad road followed by the crowded highway that led to Los Angeles. We arrived in Altadena, a suburb of Los Angeles, our final destination, around nine in the evening after a journey of eight days.

CHAPTER 25

Home in Los Angeles, California

OUR NEW HOME IN Altadena, a suburb of Los Angeles, was close to the California Institute of Technology, known as "Caltech," where Joe would be working for the next three months. We rented a house from a professor who was also away on sabbatical; Ginnie reminds me it was at 126 Morada Drive.

The house, cool and gracious, was built in Spanish style with a red roof, and surrounded by many different kinds of trees: lemon, orange, grapefruit, pomegranate, almond, and palm. The vegetable garden was messy—the owners had been away for a while—but over the next weeks, Joe and I raked and weeded it into order. One day when we were busy in the garden, a woman showed up at the house. She introduced herself as a friend of the owners of the house, and I suspect she was checking us out as renters. She was also, as it turned out, the ex-wife of George Beadle, a former president of the University of Chicago. Perhaps because we were clearly working in the garden when she called by, we must have passed muster.

The house had three bedrooms, a living room, a kitchen, a large garden with palm trees in front, and a vegetable patch at the back. It was close to the local public school where we registered the girls. Although it was no Lab School, the place was adequate, and had a large concrete playground where the girls joined in games of hopscotch and rope skipping. They walked to school every morning by way of a lane that wound through an orange grove, the air sweet with perfume. At the end of the first day of school, Virginia couldn't find me and decided to walk home alone. She became lost, and remembers the incident vividly because she wandered about for several hours in drenching rain knocking on doors. At first, every person who replied to her knock was a Mexican maid who had no English, and it was an hour before she found one who understood her. Meanwhile, I was becoming anxious, until one of the maids phoned to let me know she had Ginnie at her door; relieved, I drove to the house to bring her home.

My only complaint about the new school concerned the absurdity of air raid drills during which the children were instructed to protect themselves from atomic bombs by cowering under their desks. In her turn, Sue was indignant when asked to write an essay titled, "Why California Is the Best State." When the children returned to the Lab School, they discovered that they had missed certain lessons, and from then on, any gaps in their knowledge were attributed to having been "away in California." But I believe all of us enjoyed our stay in the West—Joe because his new colleagues were first class, all of us because we were able to visit, in addition to the Pacific Ocean, the many fascinating parks from California as far north as Washington State, and east into Arizona and New Mexico.

The Caltech staff welcomed us, as did my friend Martha Clayton's parents, Professor and Mrs. Bacher, who invited us to their home in Pasadena where we swam in their pool beneath blossoming lemon trees. We spent most weekends and school holidays driving to state parks where we camped and hiked. Our first adventure was to return to the Grand Canyon, where Joe and I, who had grown up in the English Pennine country with its low hills and lush green valleys, still could not believe what we were seeing. We were awed by the sheer immensity of the canyon, the depth of its cliff faces, the subtle colors of its sedimentary rock, its huge, flat mesas to east and west, its many desert plants, and, deep beneath us, glimpses of the winding Colorado River. Over the millennia, its rushing waters had worn away the rock to form this glorious panorama. We strolled along the edge of the canyon's south face, and for a while followed a precipitous path that led down a mile or more to its floor. More adventurous visitors were riding down on sure-footed mules, but the path was steep and winding in the extreme; because of that and the ankle-deep mule droppings, we gave up and climbed back up the path to walk along the rim.

Once, while driving on a highway "cloverleaf" in L.A. en route to Wildrose Canyon in Death Valley, California, we lost a sleeping bag off our car roof. Immediately after, we saw a group of people on motorcycles chasing us on the freeway and pointing to our car. Of course, we had no idea what they were doing, and it was a little discombobulating, to say the least. When we arrived at the camp, we realized our loss, and Ginnie and Susan had to double up in one sleeping bag.

We found ourselves to be the only people in the campground. That night, we lay in our sleeping bags without tents in a hillside cleft, looking up into the immense darkness, marveling at the number of stars. They seemed so close to the earth we felt we could have plucked them like jewels from their surrounding velvet.

Later that night, a lone car appeared that drove slowly around the camp, stopping at every site before moving on to the next. *This is it*, I thought. *Mr. Powers's Bad Guys of the West are casing the joint, planning to rob us!* We alerted the girls, and they and I retreated to the tent, where I stood on guard at the entrance, holding the only weapon I could find, a small English cricket bat we had brought with us, while Joe, armed with a large shovel, hid behind a nearby rock ready to pounce. When at last the car stopped at our tent, a passenger disembarked and produced the anticlimax: "Hi, folks. You seen a car with Indiana plates?" It turned out he was supposed to meet some friends so they could camp together. We hastily put away the shovel and the cricket bat and pretended to be normal.

In the morning, we were roused by a group of wild horses, hooves clattering close to us among the pebbles as they foraged for food along the arroyo. Later in the day, we only just managed to escape out of the desert when a following wind immobilized the car's fan and caused the engine to overheat until it was in danger of stopping altogether. With few other travelers on the road, and temperatures over one hundred degrees Fahrenheit, had the car stalled we could have been roasted to death. Obviously, the car didn't stall.

On our trip to the Painted Desert in Arizona, we discovered real "badlands," with little vegetation among its tepee-shaped hills, composed of white limestone, pink sandstone, and darker areas of volcanic rock, all of which gave the landscape its painted appearance. Continuing south, we visited the huge petrified redwood trees in Petrified Forest National Park, which looked exactly as though they had been chopped down the day before, their massive trunks left to lie on the floor of the desert. Millions of years before, when that part of the land lay at the equator, these had been live trees; now, from the bark inward, silica minerals had replaced everything and the fallen trunks looked as though they had been sculpted from darkened glass.

The area was fascinating to Joe the mineralogist, to me as a budding rock hound, and to the girls, who had an exciting time climbing, probably illegally, over and around the rock-like trees. We walked among the fallen giants for some time, only to discover when we returned to our car that some real western bad guys had stolen one of our suitcases from its roof. I wondered what they had expected to find, and how they reacted when they opened the case to find it full of the children's dirty laundry.

One weekend, we drove south to Joshua Tree National Park in the Mojave Desert, where there were small forests, and single trees scattered here and there in the sand. Joshua trees have narrow, bristling trunks, and their branches, with yucca-like leaves clustered at the top, look as though they are raising their hands to the heavens, like Joshua supplicating God. The geology is extremely complicated, consisting of rocks aged between 1.7 and 2.5 billion years old, including everything from schist, gneiss, and granite to sedimentary rock. In the area of the park we visited were what looked like huge hardened bubbles of granite piled precariously on top of each other.

Another weekend we took a trip to Sequoia National Park, where the coastal redwoods surrounded us; enormous living trees some thousands of years old. Their trunks had reddish bark, and some of them were ninety feet in circumference and up to three hundred feet tall; a road leads through one of them. We also visited Yosemite National Park, founded by the combined efforts of the famous naturalist John Muir and President Teddy Roosevelt. Both parks are in the Sierra Nevada Mountains in the east of the state, with its famous valley on the Merced River above which rears the high, rounded "Half Dome," one of the Yosemite's most famous granite cliffs, with streams cascading down its face to join the river in the valley below. The air was misty, but we camped and awoke the next morning to find the day lovely as we drove through the valley.

A trip south, down the California coast, introduced us to an element of California we had read about but hitherto never come across. At San Diego, we stopped for lunch before turning east into the hills where Joe hoped to examine a roadside outcropping he had been told about. We were late when he finished wielding his hammer, and having decided to stay the night, we found an isolated hotel back in the hills. When we entered the lobby, there was no one about: no visitors, no employees, no one staffing the desk. We waited, we hit the bell and waited some more: nothing. Finally, after about ten minutes a young man appeared through a swing door behind the counter, came in and leaned languidly against it. He was tall, his long dark hair tied back in a ponytail, his t-shirt full of holes.

"Do for ya?" he wanted to know. A real, laid-back Californian, I decided. We explained that we wanted a room, at which he took a deep breath, and shook his head.

"We're kinda full right now."

Joe looked doubtful. "Where is everybody, then?" He pointed out that there was no one in the lobby but us, and that the nearby lounge and restaurant were empty, even though it was dinnertime.

"Yeah, well," the clerk said vaguely, looking around. "Yeah."

Silently, we contemplated the empty hall. After a moment, another youth arrived through the door behind the counter. This one was small, his skull shaved, a tattoo of a serpent graced his neck, and he too wore jeans and a torn t-shirt. He waved to us, and sat down heavily on a stool behind the counter.

"Hi, there!" In case we hadn't noticed, he waved again, and I began to wonder if he was drunk.

"These guys want a room," Pony Tail informed him. They looked at each other, and exchanged a grin.

"I guess there's cabana 14," Serpent admitted, and I wondered what it was about the cabana that amused both men. But it was late, the girls were drooping, and we were a long way from San Diego, so I nudged Joe and said we would take it. Again, the two exchanged glances, and one even shook his head at the other; nevertheless, Pony Tail handed Joe a key and pointed out a dark path leading toward a small wood and a group of cottages. We stumbled down the path, found number fourteen, and entered.

The man in the bed seemed not at all startled. He sat up, and like the youth in the lobby, gave us a friendly wave before scrambling from the bed. "I'm leavin', I'm leavin'," he assured us. He was wearing a pair of boxers that weren't quite doing their job, and as he climbed into a pair of jeans, Joe and I looked at each other and decided that San Diego wasn't so far away after all; we hightailed it out of there. When the next day Joe told our story at the lab, there was much hilarity among his colleagues as they informed him that our chosen hotel was a well-known hangout for druggies.

CHAPTER 26

Homeward Bound

BETWEEN ALL THESE EXCURSIONS, Joe's research was going well at Caltech, the girls had settled into their routine at school, and I was enjoying being a Californian for a while. But by June 1965, our three months on the West Coast were coming to an end, and soon it would be time to choose our route back to Chicago. Caltech had offered Joe a position at the university, but we had found the air so bad, and Joe's allergies so much worse than in Illinois (despite Hyde Park's beige air), that he declined. However, we were determined not to leave the West before introducing the girls to Yellowstone National Park, which we had visited in 1952, so instead of going home the way we had come, we took a different direction: Route 101 North.

We approached San Francisco through more miles of breathtaking redwood trees that soared above us, their trunks massive, their crowns unbelievably far above our heads. We stayed the night in a lodge, and the next morning continued north to Yosemite National Park through weather I declared "Walter Scotty." Despite the damp evening, we camped for the night, and cooked dinner on a fire before retiring to our tent. The next day was sunny, so we took a horseback ride through that serene valley.

It took two hours, and afterward I declared that on horseback I felt "like a Marlboro ad."

The drive to San Francisco took us through more miles of redwood forests, followed by rolling prairie. I found San Francisco a lovely town, with very clean, pink and white houses, on hills overlooking the bay and the Pacific Ocean. Joe was busy talking science with an acquaintance most of the day, so the girls and I took a ride on one of the famous trolley cars. In the late nineteenth century, these trams had been the inspiration for the one back home in Matlock, Derbyshire, which transported visitors up a precipitous hill to the hydros (spas) where they could take the waters. The hill, known as Bank Road, has a 1 in 3½ ft. gradient. The tram put my grandfather's broughams and horses, which he used to transport visitors up the hill to the hydros, out of business.

We rode down to Fisherman's Wharf where we visited a nineteenth-century cargo ship, the Balclutha, and a World War II submarine; having visited one in Portsmouth, England, I knew my claustrophobia would flare up if we took the tour. Instead, we had lunch at a wharf-side restaurant where we could watch the sea lions cavorting below us, or flopping lazily about the quay. In the evening, we accompanied Joe and some of his colleagues to the famous "hungry i" restaurant, which I voted "Hyde Parkish, but cleaner," and the district as having "interesting arty stores with lots of Beatnik types around." The next day we took a boat ride that went under the beautiful Golden Gate Bridge, and afterward visited the Japanese tea garden, followed by the university's horticultural research station. The day was sunny and breezy, and I decided I really loved the town. In the evening, we ate dinner at the Wharf, and afterward took a cable car to the top of Monument Hill where we enjoyed the glorious pink-and-yellow stained sky as the sun went down over the Pacific.

The next day, we drove to Lassen Volcanic National Park in northern California, through a mountain pass with twenty inches of snow on either side. Beyond the snow, we stayed at a motel in Falls River Mills, and in the morning found the surrounding hills to be covered in juniper and the air full of the scent of damp sage that reminded me of Scottish bog myrtle.

Then it was on to Oregon, where Joe had learned that there were lava tunnels—known as tubes—which formed thousands of years ago when active volcanoes spewed out liquid basalt that flowed downhill. The heat of this outflow was enormous, but eventually the top layer cooled and solidified forming a crust, leaving the hotter lava to continue flowing underneath. When the volcanoes became inactive, the last of the molten lava drained away and left behind the tubes where our daughters shrieked and ran.

Oregon is home to hundreds of these tubes. The one we visited was close to the coast, and hundreds of meters long. We rented lanterns and plunged into the tunnel. The roof was so high that claustrophobia was not a problem; the temperature was a comfortable forty-seven degrees. Walking was easy and the children ran ahead, marveling as their shouts echoed off the surrounding walls. When at last we saw light at the end of the tunnel and emerged into sunshine, we found beneath us the Pacific

Ocean, blue and turbulent, the rock under our feet gritty with crushed lava.

It was on this trip north that we came across a cattle truck that had been hit by another vehicle, scattering dead or injured cattle across the road. Joe, ever the farmer's boy, immediately hopped out of the car, and went to help drag dead cattle from the road and round up those that had wandered away. Meanwhile, the girls and I looked in the opposite direction, trying to block out the sight of blood, and the sound of animals in pain.

Further north, near the Oregon-Washington border, we came across a visitor center honoring J. Harlen Bretz, a professor at the University of Chicago who, along with a colleague, proposed that the nearby landscape had been scoured by flood water, leaving behind rocky shelves of which one was the site of the earth's largest waterfall. Huge boulders—glacial erratics that were rafted in on icebergs—littered the area. Bretz called the region "The Channeled Scablands." He challenged the standard explanation that glaciers had carved out the landscape, and proposed that during the Ice Age, about fifteen thousand years ago, an ice dam broke, causing a sudden catastrophic draining of Glacial Lake Missoula that sculpted the landscape in a mere two to three days. Bretz claimed that the water must have traveled at speeds approaching sixty miles per hour. After enduring more than fifty years of ridicule for his theory, Bretz was finally vindicated in 1979 when his work was publicly acknowledged. He was ninety-seven.

Heading southeast toward Idaho, the weather changed again, and a torrential storm swept in from the west. The pounding of rain on the roof of the car, plus the smell of sage, made me report, "raining like blazes—it smells, and even sounds like Scotland." There were many small deserted farms in the area, and ghost mining towns; this had been gold-mining country during the last century. We found the area to be less of a tourist mecca, the countryside open and grassy with lovely wide meadows. We booked into a dude ranch where moose came close to our cabin during the night. The next day we took another horseback ride, this time accompanied by what I termed "a very amiable wrangler." It was a beautiful day, fresh and clear, and we rode in upland meadows filled with yellow daisies and blue lupines; aspens newly in leaf trembled in the breeze. At an overlook, we dismounted, and walked along the rim from where we could see an osprey nest far below and a mother bird feeding her young. The ride to the overlook and back took two hours. Afterward, we took a jouncing stagecoach ride of about fifteen minutes, which made our behinds as painful as both our horseback rides combined. "Thank goodness for Henry Ford?" I wrote. You'll note that I added a question mark.

As we drove toward Craters of the Moon National Monument in Idaho, the scenery changed again, the lava areas gradually giving way to low hills that reminded me of both Wisconsin and Derbyshire. There were green areas with some juniper and sage, but the irrigated valleys were reserved chiefly for potatoes and fields full of horses. We arrived at Craters of the Moon at sunset. There we again found ourselves surrounded by volcanic cones, some snow covered, which were part of the massive flow of ancient lava that covers the northernmost part of Idaho, the largest volcanic area in the contiguous United States. The ground was covered in a jumble of rocks that made the area seem as desiccated and featureless as the surface of the moon.

Further south again, we traveled through scrubby pine forests to Idaho's capital, Boise, a thriving little town with art galleries, a museum, and many small parks. It is situated in a green valley surrounded by bare, snowy mountains. As we left, the lava hills purple in the evening light, we drove over a pass between walls of snow that towered twenty feet on either side.

The weather was cold for June, but the air was fresh when we arrived at Arco, Idaho, a town powered by atomic energy from a nearby reactor belonging to Argonne National Lab, in Illinois. The nearby countryside was buried in tall sagebrush. We had hoped to camp in the Tetons, but the campsite was jammed with tourists and mosquitoes; nevertheless, as we drove away, we again enjoyed the glorious mountain scenery, the summits pink in the sunset.

Then it was on to Yellowstone Park where we again saw elk, bears, and mountain sheep. The surrounding mountains and lakes were as lovely, and Old Faithful as exciting as I remembered from our first trip. The water began to spout at 1:00 p.m., fortuitously it turned out. We had been led to expect such activity at one o'clock each day, but it turned out that the geyser actually spouts every ninety minutes, or even less when the previous spout has involved more water. We took a cabin near Old Faithful, and from there renewed our acquaintance with various mud pots and hot springs, and took yet another horse ride to a nearby falls. We amateur riders forded two rivers, one of them very swift; afterward, the girls and I were so saddle sore we could hardly stand.

We continued on to Lander, Wyoming, and to Sinks Canyon State Park where the river literally sinks beneath the valley floor. This was limestone country, a porous land like that of Derbyshire, where rivers often flow through underground tunnels. Spring flowers surrounded us, including irises and ragwort, and above the river were masses of sunflowers, lupines, and phlox.

The next town was Casper, Wyoming, about which I wrote, "A ghastly place—and we're now getting East, alas and alack!"

But the next day was lovely, though hot, and on the way to Ogallala, Nebraska we visited Fort Laramie, which, although it was a historic area, looked like a military camp from no earlier than World War II. The officers' quarters, gracious white wooden buildings, had been reconstructed and given faintly Victorian furniture. We saw much flooding along the Platte River. The area had recently had more rain in two days than they normally have in a year. At Ogallala, we stayed in a motel with a pool, had a refreshing swim and dinner in town, after which we visited an excellent western museum, and a rather tawdry Sioux trading post.

As we drove through Nebraska to Manhattan, Kansas, the country became flatter, although still with rolling hills and acres of sunflowers; the western mountains had been left behind. Manhattan is the site of the State University, the pleasant campus reminding us of Penn State. The surrounding countryside had vast wheat and cornfields, and many herds of cattle.

Kansas City was a pleasant, clean little town, I decided, "though a trifle hicky." I'm not sure what I meant by that since an imposing building housed a very handsome art gallery with a good selection of both modern and traditional arts.

I found the roadside in Missouri to be messy with billboards and junkyards, and by the time we arrived in Carbondale, Illinois, the country areas had become "scrubby." We visited Merrimac Cave, which "was a vast mistake," though my journal doesn't say why that was. We saw two old friends in Carbondale, Mike and Hilary Bown from Cambridge, England, who were visiting another old friend, Don Bloss, a professor at the local university.

Rather than head straight back to Chicago from Carbondale, we drove south through Kentucky to Tennessee for Joe to meet with a fellow scientist. In Kentucky, we found green, pleasantly rolling countryside, with deciduous trees, and lots of honeysuckle and tiger lilies. We visited Mammoth National Park in limestone country, the cave full of stalagmites and stalactites, and were given an "excellent explanation of the geology"—a clue to why the visit to the Merrimac Cave had been a disaster. (I assume the previous cave had been what I felt was "Disneyfied.")

At Gatlinburg, Tennessee, we enjoyed a glorious view of the Smoky Mountains, their meadows awash in brown-eyed Susans. The forests were full of deciduous trees; I think I must have missed them when we were among the western pine forests. Joe met with a colleague in Gatlinburg, after which we turned around and drove north, finally arriving back at our home in Hyde Park.

Our trip west had been a breathtaking adventure, the mountain and desert vistas glorious beyond belief. I have visited beyond the Mississippi only a few times since then, and may not again, but the memories of those days are vivid, the pictures they conjure for me both exciting and consoling.

CHAPTER 27

The East Coast

IN 1968, WE TOOK a break from our annual summer trips to England, and headed off to investigate the East Coast of America. I don't remember why we made this decision, but it caused resentment with the children, because they loved their English summers on Birchwood Farm and spending time with their paternal Smith grandparents, their maternal Wallis grandmother, and their uncles, aunts, and cousins. It didn't help that I arranged for them to go to summer school and take typing lessons in the early part of the summer. Most of my typing was of the "hunt-and-peck" variety, and I wanted my daughters to have better preparation for college.

When we lived in Washington, DC, in the early fifties, most of our trips had been to various historic sites: Antietam, Monticello, and John Brown's bailiwick in the Shenandoah Valley. Now we decided to take a look at the northeast, particularly along the coast.

We began our investigation of New England in the north, at Acadia National Park on the coast of Maine, where there were few sand beaches, but glorious tumbles of rock where the sea sucked and gurgled; at high tide the waters roared like thunder. Further out to sea were rocky islands where gulls and cormorants glided, the whole panorama reminding me of the west coast of Scotland.

In Acadia, Joe found a raccoon with its nose caught in a tin it had been nuzzling for food and, practical man that he was, he managed to free it without getting bitten.

After Acadia, we visited Old Sturbridge Village in central Massachusetts, which dates from the seventeenth and eighteenth centuries. The village included a farm—which the children loved—plus mills on its small river, a covered bridge, a blacksmith's shop, and a Quaker house where we watched wool being spun into yarn. I wondered if this village had any connection to the Quakers who lived in my home village in Derbyshire, since many of them emigrated from there to Pennsylvania, and Sturbridge in western Massachusetts.

Returning to the Massachusetts coast, we found a great deal of history—rather more than the tales of Indian tribes and adventure-seeking Frenchmen, which had been all the history the Midwest around Chicago had to offer.

I was fascinated by Boston's history, dating from 1630, even though most of it reveals England in a bad light. There was the Boston Tea Party in 1773, when colonists, dressed as Indians, tossed shiploads of tea into the sea to protest the large tax the British had put on it. On April 19, 1775, the first battle of the Revolutionary War between the colonials and the British Red Coats took place in Lexington and Concord. Paul Revere and two others rode from Boston to warn that "the British are coming!" This was soon followed on June 17 by the Battle of Bunker Hill. A year later, British troops were forced to withdraw from Boston when, after years of fighting, King George III finally relinquished his claim to the Thirteen Colonies. The United States won its independence in 1783.

We walked Boston's Freedom Trail, which was established after a suggestion in the fifties by journalist William Schofield that there be a marked path to many of the major events that took place in Boston during the American Revolution. This two-and-a-half mile redbrick path begins on Boston Common and proceeds as far as Charlestown, where the USS Constitution is docked. The sixteen historic sites include the Old South Meeting House, the Paul Revere House, and the Old North Church, where we sat for a while in its high-walled, boxed pews, with their padded benches and ladder-backed chairs. The church is built of red brick, with a white, wooden steeple. Inside, the walls are whitewashed, and the windows have plain glass. At my secondary school in England, we were given only one term to cover American history; after visiting Boston I knew we had been shortchanged.

We ventured further west in Massachusetts. My daughter Virginia remembers the magnificent gates at the entrance to Smith, a top women's college in Northampton, and reminds me that her father urged her and Susan to apply to Smith when the time came for them to choose a university. Neither of our daughters did, but Ginnie's daughter Katie later went to Smith.

On that same trip, we made a stop in State College, Pennsylvania, where we visited our old friends, Lisa and Len Herzog. That evening their son, Fritz, took the girls, who were fourteen and thirteen, to his room to show off his new Ouija board while Joe and I sat in the kitchen and talked of old times with Lisa and Len.

As Ginnie told me later, Fritz settled them and his younger sister Heather and brother Clayton around the board, and Ginnie and Heather placed their fingers lightly on the planchette (the slider), and then all lights were extinguished. Slowly, the slider began to move, stopping at various letters in turn. Whenever it stopped, Fritz turned on a flashlight to reveal the letter. The letters *H, A, T, E, S, F, O, O, D* were revealed, and the slider moved no more. At that point, Clay, then five years old, started rocking and moaning. Apparently, many years before, a young boy of the same age had choked to death in the kitchen. The children looked warily at one another; was the spirit of the deceased boy trying to communicate with them through the Ouija board? Fritz, and indeed, all the children, were convinced that he was the source of the message, "Hates Food." Ginnie and Heather claimed that they had not controlled the slider, and because the room was totally dark until the slider stopped and a flashlight was produced, what other explanation was there? I, the skeptic, was not convinced. Fritz now works in Hollywood, and if he's not producing macabre thrillers, he ought to be.

In the early nineties, Joe and I made a return trip to State College. We stayed at the Nittany Lion Inn, and while Joe was busy talking rocks and minerals with his colleagues, I took a walk down to our old house and was happy to find that it looked exactly as I remembered. It was spring, and the old apple trees, in full bloom, were still there. I knew the girls would be happy to receive a photo of their old home, but unfortunately, I had forgotten to take my camera. The hotel was only a few blocks away, so I walked back to get it. While I was there, Joe returned for lunch. I described to him what I had seen, and he decided to come with me to see the old house and the apple blossoms. When we arrived on Hamilton Avenue, we found the current owners of the house busy in the garden. In the two hours I'd been away, they had reduced their lovely apple trees to stumps, and were busy chopping the trunks and branches into firewood. I took no photographs that day.

CHAPTER 28

Visitors

ALMOST ALL OF THE trips my family took were to visit our family in England, but after my father died in 1963, my mother came to live with us in Chicago for nine months. It was a wonderful time for the girls, but a great worry for me, because my mother had no sense of the danger of the streets, and wandered into some uninhabited areas of parkland near Lake Michigan. Thankfully, she remained unscathed by Chicago street crime, but unfortunately she stepped off a curb outside our house soon after arriving, and fell and broke her wrist. She was put in a cast, and a funny one it was, with an unnatural bend at the wrist. She had broken her other wrist many years earlier in England, and had been put in a normal straight cast. However, despite her skepticism, when her wrist was released from the bendy cast, it had healed beautifully, and she had no more trouble with it, unlike her other wrist.

She came again in 1968, adding to our family happiness, but during each of her visits, there was a national tragedy involving members of the Kennedy family. On November 22, 1963, President John F. Kennedy, the young, handsome, American leader, was assassinated in Dallas. Then on June 5, 1968, while running for president, JFK's brother, Senator Robert F. Kennedy, was shot in Los Angeles while campaigning and died the next day.

My mother visited us one last time in 1975, accompanied by my cousin, Janet Durward. I breathed a sense of relief that, that time, the Kennedy family escaped unscathed.

In the late sixties, Joe's parents flew to Canada to visit Joe's brother Tom and family; Joe and I volunteered to drive up to meet them and bring them back to Chicago with us. Upon their arrival in Montreal, they took a room in a motel while they waited for us to pick them up the next day. While they were sleeping, thieves broke into their room and stole all their cash. Not a pleasant introduction to the New World. Joe decided to take them to Chicago via what he thought would be a scenic route along the northern shores of Lake Huron, which he thought would have the benefit of keeping his parents' time in Chicago to a bare minimum. He figured that his parents would dislike being trapped in a city, especially one so sprawling and fraught with danger as the South Side of Chicago.

As far as Joe's father was concerned, the trip around the lake was an unfortunate choice: "nothing but blooming trees," he complained as we drove mile after endless mile. And no, he didn't mean the trees were in flower. We looked for animals to keep Granddad interested: deer, moose, bears. But no, as we drove along the dark, narrow roads, trees arching tunnel-like overhead, we found no furry company. Finally, in desperation, Joe took a turn off the main highway onto an even narrower road that led toward the lake, where at last we came across a bear with a couple of cubs. As far as Granddad was concerned, they didn't make up for the extra half a mile of boring trees.

After that we turned south into the state of Wisconsin, and for the first time on this side of the Atlantic, Granddad Smith smiled. Here was his kind of country: open green hills, cows, sheep, crops, farming! Heaven at last! He loved the countryside all the way to the outskirts of Chicago. When we reached Chicago, he seemed so delighted to finally be in one place that any of the city's deficiencies paled in comparison to the endless forests of the Great Lakes.

A year later, it was Joe's aunt Alice's turn to visit. Auntie Al was a great favorite of us all. We took her to visit friends who had places in the country, on walks as far as Wooded Island behind the Museum of Science and Industry, and to The Point, where she loved to sit on a bench beside me and watch the children jump from one large boulder to the next.

Auntie Al had never married but loved children. We always assumed she was single because she was of the generation that saw the bulk of its young menfolk killed during the First World War. She made a fuss of the girls and seemed delighted with everything she saw in America, unaware of the mayhem that surrounded the university. On our trips to The Point, she never seemed to notice the sinister metal towers surrounded by a low wall that took up one section of that lakeside park. The towers belonged to a radar site constructed by the army in the fifties as part of the Cold War defense system. It was dismantled in 1971, which made the Point a more appealing park jutting into Lake Michigan.

Auntie Alice's greatest claim to fame, at least in our family, was her derring-do with Charlie, a cockerel that Sue had brought home from school. When small, he ran about the patio pecking at my petunias and was easily corralled, but by the time of our aunt's visit he was a fully-grown rooster that spent his nights in our basement perched on the back of an old chair thick with his droppings. In the mornings, his strident cock-a-doodle-doos could be heard all the way up the stairs. Charlie, a Rhode Island Red, had grown into a handsome bird, his scarlet comb a flag of triumph.

Susan reminds me that before she took over Charlie from the seniors at her high school, they had injected him with testosterone, hence his outsize comb, his resplendent wattles, and his huge libido. When she let him out into the patio, she had to watch carefully in case he escaped. One day when Sue was at school he did so. Auntie Al, farming background to the fore, chased him down the avenue and came back triumphant, carrying him by his feet, a most unusual sight in the confines of a big city. Not long after that a local official came to inform me that chickens of any kind were not allowed in Hyde Park. (Both hens and cockerels are called chickens in the United States.) He promised to send someone to collect Charlie, assuring us that he would be well looked after on a farm. I had my doubts, but Sue was young enough to be trusting.

CHAPTER 29

Over the Moon

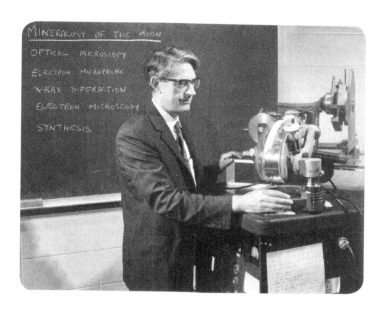

THE APOLLO MOON LANDING by American astronauts, in July 1969, was an exciting time for us all, but particularly for Joe who, as a young boy in England, standing in his father's fields at night, had gazed up at the moon, noting the black and white areas on its surface. Later, this young rock hound became one of the principal investigators for NASA's Apollo 11 spaceflight. Michael Collins piloted the commanded spacecraft, while his colleagues Neil Armstrong and Buzz Aldrin set foot on this new world. Joe and his team of scientists studied the moon rocks after they were returned to earth by the expedition. And I had the thrill of holding a slide with a piece of the moon in my hands.

Joe subsequently identified the first new mineral from the moon as pyroxferroite, and reported on it at the first Lunar and Planetary Science Conference in 1970. It was at that meeting that he also put forward his "hot moon" hypothesis: that the moon had once been molten. As it cooled, the feldspar-rich andesite rose to form light-colored highlands. Later, during periods of volcanism, dark basaltic lava erupted to form the maria, or seas. This explained the dark and light areas his younger self had noted on the moon's surface.

Harold Urey, an eminent alumnus of the University of Chicago's Department of Geophysical Sciences, scorned this idea, saying that he didn't know how anyone from his old university "dared propose such a ridiculous scheme." Urey had earlier proposed his "cold moon" theory, in which the maria was thought to consist of the solidified remains of large bodies of molten rock that were created by collisions with meteorites or asteroids. However, when the moon rocks from the Apollo 11 mission were analyzed, they were discovered to be basalts, which were formed volcanically. Urey's "cold moon" theory was disproved, and today, most scientists think that Joe was right and Urey wrong.

I wrote a poem about Joe's "hot moon" theory for the "Howard B. Zar Hot Moon Rock Jingle Contest," that was published in the afore-mentioned DOGSheet. I wrote it in honor of our daughters, who rarely saw their father when he was deeply involved in his work on the moon rocks, and dedicated it to "moon orphans everywhere!"

The Plaint of the Moon Orphan

"Oh Mother dear," the orphan cries,
"Is Father coming soon?"
"Hush now, my love,"
His dam replies,
"He's coping with the moon!"

"He has moon rocks of the finest sort,
of color red and yellow,
And now he's writing his report—
No use for you to bellow!"

"My Daddy says the moon was hot,
Will fame and fortune follow?"
"The others say, 'Oh no, t'was not!'
Depends whose tale you swallow."

"But hush-a-bye, my little lad,
And as you dream remember,
If 13* doesn't leave the pad,
You'll see him, come November!"

* Apollo 13, the seventh manned mission in the Apollo space program.

Because of his work with the moon rocks, Joe was asked by the Field Museum of Natural History in Chicago to help display some of the specimens supplied by NASA. This he did, and the museum and NASA mounted an exhibition that attracted crowds of viewers. One visitor was Jane Byrne, then working for Mayor Richard Daley, who was most insistent that she needed to touch one of the specimens. Joe, of course refused; germs from her fingers would have contaminated the rocks and made them unsuitable for further research. As it happened he had with him a thin section of a specimen, a shaving of rock enclosed between two glass slides to prevent contamination, which he had put aside having decided it was too small for the exhibit. This he held out to Ms. Byrne, as he had earlier to me; she touched the glass reverently, eyes closed as if in prayer. Her prayer appears to have been answered because, in 1979 she became the first woman to be elected Mayor of Chicago.

CHAPTER 30

The Seventies

THE 1960S WITNESSED RIOTS in many large American cities after the assassinations of the black Muslim leader, Malcolm X, on February 21, 1965, and of the towering civil-rights leader, Dr. Martin Luther King Jr., on April 4, 1968. Dr. King led peaceful marches—peaceful, that is, until the police unleashed snarling dogs on the demonstrators, or white groups attacked the marchers. In the four hundred years since the first Africans were brought on slave ships to America, African Americans have been, and continue to be, discriminated against in so many areas—schooling, employment, housing, health care,

173

you name it. I can well understand why blacks rioted on the streets of large cities, after centuries of discrimination and the assassinations of civil rights leaders.

The burgeoning feminist movement also added to the turbulence in American society, beginning in 1962 with the publication of Betty Friedan's *The Feminine Mystique.* The establishment of the National Organization for Women (NOW), and the debut of *Ms.* magazine in 1972, under the leadership of the feminist Gloria Steinem, served to bring discrimination against women to the fore. Women were, and continue to be, discriminated against in employment, with many careers not open to them, no matter how talented. Sexual abuse and assaults were frequent, and many times not investigated by law enforcement who said that the woman was herself at fault for the assault.

And there was the ongoing and escalating war in Vietnam. Few people understood why America sent troops to fight in Vietnam in the first place, especially in the face of atrocities such as the My Lai Massacre in 1968, in which more than five hundred men, women, and children were killed by an American Army company, and the My Khe massacre, also in 1968, in which between eighty and ninety civilians were killed by American military. Richard Nixon was a deeply unpopular president; the will of the people was to extricate America from Vietnam; but still, the war dragged on, killing over fifty-eight thousand American troops, and hundreds of thousands of Vietnamese troops and civilians.

In Chicago and throughout the United States, there were many protest marches against the war in Vietnam, where US combat troops were first deployed in 1965; by 1968, there were over five hundred thousand American troops in Vietnam. Joe and I, and our friends, Sue and David Zesmer, took part in one of the antiwar protests. We marched the seven miles from Hyde Park to downtown Chicago through the black neighborhoods, watched silently by the people we passed. There were police at every intersection, some of whom, probably fed up with having to do extra work, harried us along. A sour note came when some protesters yelled insults at a group of US sailors watching from the sidewalk. Joe shouted at them to stop; the sailors were not responsible for the war. On August 28, 1968, during the Democratic National Convention in downtown Chicago where Senator Hubert H. Humphrey, the Democratic candidate for president, was to be nominated, there were violent protests in the streets, with Chicago police officers brutally beating protestors' heads with batons. Joe, I, and the girls watched with horror the scene unfolding on television only a few miles from where we lived.

Protest gatherings became even more violent in May 1970 after a local militia fired on a peaceful antiwar student demonstration at Kent State University in Ohio, killing four students and wounding nine. Eleven days later, at Jackson State University, in Mississippi, city and state police fired on students, killing two, and wounding twelve. Violence had arrived on US campuses.

More locally, students took to the streets when the University of Chicago handed over their grades to the military, which could affect whether or not they would be drafted. When these gatherings became more violent, a university court was convened to discipline the students, and Joe joined a group of faculty who filled every alternate seat in the room in case of trouble. One student asked Joe, threateningly, if his wife ever walked alone in Hyde Park. Joe did not reply, but took a sheet of paper on which the list of students attending the meeting were printed, and, showing it to the student, pointed out the youth's name. The youth immediately left the meeting, but subsequently I always stayed at home after dark, and was careful even in daylight for a while.

In the midst of all this turbulence, I had a brief respite while something of beauty was created at the University of Chicago's Rockefeller Chapel.

Built between 1925 and 1928 and funded by robber baron Nelson Rockefeller, the Chapel was large enough to accommodate seventeen hundred people, its tower the tallest structure on the University of Chicago campus. In addition to weekly Christian services, there were concerts and lectures, and, more recently, services for people of other beliefs. Above the altar is a stained-glass window in soft greens, blues, and mauves in the shape of a rose that was designed by the architect, Bertram Grosvenor Goodhue.

A series of smaller lancet windows, titled "The Ten Creation Windows," were designed by U of C Professor Harold Haydon in the early seventies, and were crafted and installed along the aisles of the Chapel. Five on the eastern wall depict the foundational elements: Heaven, Air, Water, Earth, and Fire; five on the western wall represent living things: Plants, Animals, Man, Woman, and The Works of the Mind. The ten windows were crafted by a small band of volunteers. Using materials and techniques developed centuries ago, they cut antique handblown colored glass from Germany into the requisite shapes and inserted them into the lead surrounds.

During the summer of 1972, between her first and second years at college, Ginnie and her high school friend Miriam Redleaf created the stained-glass window for "The Works of the Mind." Several volunteers, including Susan and Miriam's younger sister, helped in the early stages, after which Miriam and Ginnie took over the project, working throughout the summer to complete it. Cutting the glass along a straight line was fairly simple, but The Works of the Mind was particularly difficult due to the intricacy of the shapes. These included representations of Pythagoras's theorem, a Greek column, *The Madonna and Child*, and a phoenix rising from the ashes.

The body of the phoenix was inspired by Henry Moore's sculpture entitled *Nuclear Energy*, which was designed to commemorate the Manhattan Project's first successful self-sustaining controlled nuclear reaction, which took place on the campus of the University of Chicago. The statue was installed at the exact location where the experiment took place in 1942. After many tries, Ginnie succeeded in carving the head of the phoenix, which included a curved beak, but the curved piece for the body was almost impossible to accomplish, because when glass is cut, it breaks in a straight line. Many times a curve cut in the glass broke off, until, after several days of work, Miriam was successful, and she and Ginnie were able to complete this window.

Miriam Redleaf and Ginnie with their "Works of the Mind."

During the following Christmas vacation, Miriam and Ginnie also completed the Graduate's Window, depicting a Möbius strip, which was installed in a narrow slit in the stone steps leading to the church basement. This, for me, and no doubt for Ginnie also, was a rare bright spot in an extremely worrisome and disruptive time.

CHAPTER 31

Getting Educated

IN SEPTEMBER 1972, GINNIE headed back to college as a sophomore at Carleton College in Northfield, Minnesota, and Susan started as a freshman at Oberlin College, in Oberlin, Ohio. A year later, I at last managed to attend college.

I chose to go to Roosevelt University, located in downtown Chicago, and serving a population of students who were more working class, foreign, and less wealthy than those at the U of C. I majored in English literature, and earned a degree at the age of forty-seven. Despite the fact that I was older by at least twenty-five years than most of the other students, they were friendly, although I found that foreign students new to the country were more so than the native born.

To young Americans I probably seemed far too ancient for such an adventure, while the foreigners saw me as another outsider like themselves. I had one or two Asian friends during those years, one from Sri Lanka, and particularly Jae Im Kim from Seoul with whom I often had lunch. One of our neighbors at Hyde Park Co-op Homes taught English at Roosevelt and gave money for a prize in English. I managed to win the prize three times, after which I desisted, embarrassed to be standing in the way of younger aspirants.

During these years, I took lessons in oil painting at a studio on 53rd Street, where I copied the works of some of the Dutch and Flemish artists of the seventeenth and eighteenth centuries. I enjoyed this venture enormously, but once I began writing, did not continue with it. Writing was my passion from the start and now, forty-odd years later, I have produced two self-published memoirs, *A Pennine Childhood* and this one, and written manuscripts for two novels, *Chimney Sweepers* and *Critchley, Derbyshire*, plus a mystery, *Death in the Dunes*.

In the 1970s, I wrote a series of articles for the News Lady column in the *Chicago Daily News*, which I am including here, as well as two poems I wrote while at Roosevelt University.

Chicago Daily News
News Lady column
Mid-Atlantic Blues
by Brenda F. Smith

"I guess you prefer living here don't you?" the American shouted above the usual Chicago cocktail party din. Two weeks later in a pub in Derbyshire, England, an old farmer plonked down his pint of bitter on the counter and told me flatly, "America's all very well, but I bet you'd rather live here."

I replied "yes" to both of them. After having grown up in England followed by fifteen years in the States that's how I am—wishy-washy.

I have found that only those Americans or Britons who have never set foot across the water can say, without hesitation, "Great place to visit, but I wouldn't want to live there." I, on the other hand, have reached such a pitch of ambivalence that the plane has to touch down at London's Heathrow or Chicago's O'Hare Field for me to begin to wish I were on the other side of the Atlantic.

I can't even make up my mind about a simple thing such as the weather. I know as well as anyone that Chicago's winters are brutal and the summers sizzlingly hot, with blizzards, tornadoes, twisters, and floods tearing the town apart between them. But after just one rainy week spent huddled in a damp farmhouse where flagstones weep, the chimney smokes, and people in enormous boots keep clomping in with buckets of mash letting in a draft, I begin to long for the warm sun of America, incredibly blue skies; crisp clean air! I remember the fruit stands, a riot of color with bushel baskets piled high with red apples, glistening flagons filled with amber cider, bins crammed with vivid orange pumpkins. And in the woods, and along the roadsides, the oaks, the sumacs, and the unbelievable blaze of maples.

Mercifully blotted out is summer in Chicago. Forgotten is the sky the color of a miner's vest on a Friday night; sidewalks clinging stickily to one's heels; perspiration trickling wetly down one's spine. But then, being an exile is something like childbirth: when it's over you remember only the good outcome.

This amnesia spreads to everything. For example, when I'm in England it seems that all my friends there are raising their children to resemble timid mice. Dressed in neat frocks or shorts, sandals and white socks, they squeak "Yes, Mummy," and at the twitch of a parental eyebrow obediently scamper off to play in the garden while their mother and I talk in peace.

That's when I begin to think of the uninhibited American children, resplendent in cut-off jeans, old and disreputable sweatshirts and sneakers, who sprawl about my living room after school noisily discussing Vietnam, race relations, or who in their class is going with whom.

"Can't you kids talk more quietly?" I'd yell after a while. Or "Take your feet off that table," and, "For Pete's sake, Sarah, stop popping that gum!" I've even been known to declare that, "Children should be seen and not heard!"

And so it goes. Over there, in the midst of Chicago's riots and general mayhem, I mutter, "This would never happen in England!"

Conversely, when I'm here I argue that the British Prime Minister should be elected, as the American President is having forgotten for the moment the corruption and graft, the padded electoral rolls.

Over there I drool for high teas with kippers, home-baked scones with strawberry jam, scalding hot tea. Suppressing meanwhile the horrid memory of cold morning toast, overcooked cabbage, custard.

Similarly, over here, I blot out the memory of rubbery American hotdogs, canned pears served with lettuce and a dollop of mayonnaise, and salivate at the thought of pumpkin pie, turkey and cranberry sauce.

Even my patriotism is ambivalent, so when someone asks me if I'm American or English, I usually answer, "Yes." As Sir Walter Scott wrote:

Breathes there the man, with soul so dead,
Who never to himself hath said,
"This is my own, my native land!"

Yes, as a matter of fact there is, except that my soul isn't dead exactly—flummoxed might be a better word.

So American and British friends, the next time you meet this expatriate at a pub or a party, don't tell her she'd be happier on this side of the Atlantic or would be better off spending her time across the water—tell her it's a lovely day instead, and she might be able to agree.

Chicago Daily News

News Lady column
A Grandson to Crow About
by Brenda F. Smith

"Mum, may I bring Charlie home after school?"

"Charlie?" I asked, stalling for time.

My daughter's pigtails stiffened with exasperation. "Oh, Mum, you haven't been listening!"

"I've been listening," I lied. "Sure, bring Charlie home if you'd like."

And if to lie is a sin, I sure got my comeuppance: Charlie turned out to be, not a small boy who could be bundled home after supper, but a fully grown, white leghorn rooster who looked as if he figured on staying.

"Susie, why on earth have you brought that chicken home!" I shrilled.

"Because you said I could," she told me. "Charlie's my science project. And he's not a chicken; he's a rooster!"

She paused for breath, and I took the opportunity to point out that we lived in a city that was no place for roosters.

Large, liquid brown eyes looked into mine. "But, Mum, I've impregnated him!"

"Imprinted." I corrected hastily.

"Imprinted him, then," she agreed. "I brought him up from practically an egg. He follows me around school, and I taught him to sit on my arm. He thinks I'm his Mum." Here, the eyes became calculating. "I guess that means you're his grandmother."

What me, Grandmother to a rooster? But what grandparent would deny a grandchild, even if his parentage was a bit dubious? "Well, okay," I told her. "Charlie may stay—for now."

That afternoon, Charlie took possession of the patio—we'd had to let him out of his cage after he told his Mum how he hated it. The first thing he did was to make a beeline for the flower border, and I had the wild hope that he'd prove to be the solution to my cut-worm problem. But Charlie had decided it was time for his ablutions, and the middle of my petunias would be the perfect spot. He spent a delightful afternoon, and was a grand fellow if you didn't care for flower borders.

When dusk approached, there was another problem: Where would Charlie sleep? As he told his Mum, it was too cold out in the patio, and he was scared of the basement. So, as a temporary experiment, he went to sleep perched precariously on a stool in my kitchen. Then I headed for bed, happily contemplating tomorrow, Saturday, a day of rest. However, at 5:00 a.m., I found myself wide awake and sitting upright as a terrible sound rent the air.

I nudged my sleeping partner. What was that? My SP opened a baleful eye. "That," he told me, was "that darned chicken your daughter brought home." Note the possessive form. Our daughter is always exclusively mine at such times.

"Rooster," I corrected huffily.

"Rooster, schmooster," he said, burying his head under the pillow. "I need my sleep!"

So there was nothing to do but get up and see if a little breakfast would quieten Charlie.

In the kitchen, he eyed me beadily as he swayed back and forth on the stool, crowing like crazy. I approached him gingerly, corn-filled hand outstretched. "Here, Charlie," I crooned. "Gooood rooster."

Whereupon, Charlie flapped his wings and flew to perch on my arm, grasping it in his cold, scaly claws.

"My golly, Charlie, I do believe I've impregnated you," I told him.

And so it seemed, because after that he would have little to do with Susie, but followed me around like a lap dog, making little loving sounds in his throat. Yes, Charlie knew which side his corn was buttered all right!

For some weeks, Charlie spent the daylight hours in that patio, happily pecking at my petunias, and crowing up a storm. It was the crowing that led to Charlie's downfall, because one morning, a rather beefy gentleman with a distinct look of City Hall appeared on my doorstep. He was kindly, but firm. "You gotta get ridda dat rooster, lady," he told me firmly "He's annoying de neighbors, and what's worse, you ain't zoned for roosters."

Not zoned for roosters? It was the beginning of the end for Charlie. "It'll break my daughter's heart," I told him, "She thinks the world of Charlie." But guess whose eyes were filled with tears when the man came to take Charlie away.

And guess who said, "Mum, what d'you think I should study for my science project, next year?"

I guess mothers are more resilient than grandmothers.

Chicago Daily News
News Lady column
PSATS
by Brenda F. Smith

It began two years ago as a low rumble as though of an approaching storm, when a cloud, no bigger than a man's hand, appeared on our horizon. It was called PSATs.

It was not, as you may suppose, an apparition from Mars, or some strange new computer language, but merely Preliminary Scholarship Aptitude Test. I say "our horizon" because preparation for college is nothing if not a family affair.

I must say, we took our PSATs with a certain nonchalance. "Set the clock for early tomorrow, Mum," our daughter said. "It's time for PSATs."

"Sure, dear," we yawned. At dinner next evening, she told us that she felt she'd done fairly well, "but I don't suppose I'll go to college, anyway. It's sort of irrelevant."

"Maybe it is, dear," we agreed. What the heck, it was two years off.

But after that somehow things began to fall apart. First, we began getting missives from the school in which Miss Feinman coyly reminded everyone that she would be giving a talk titled, "College, Yay or Nay." Another teacher, trying hard to be with it, announced, "College tonight, gang. Telling it like it is."

Dutifully, we gathered ourselves together and attended every rap session that came our way. We learned a lot of stuff we already knew, such as colleges like it if you do well in school, and if you know the President of the school, the Admissions Office will hate you to mention it, but by golly it will get you in.

Then, a young fellow who looked as though he was just out of grade school, informed us that he was our daughter's Counselor, that there was only one place for every student who applied, but not to get uptight about it. He told us twice, at which point we parents began to get uptight about it.

So we began to buy books, such as "How to Get Your Child into College." These gave us much information, most of it conflicting, but they were agreed that colleges are always exclusive or very exclusive. Not one of them is a pushover. Now, even though she had done well with her PSATs, the plaintive cry, "I won't get in anywhere," would rend the air, and long hours were spent on the phone while she and her friends discussed the merits of colleges that would refuse them anyway. Consequently, our phone bill became almost as unbelievable as her father's language when he wrote the check.

Then, after a summer vacation "looking at colleges," all of which were voted "Icksville," we found ourselves back at square one: "college is irrelevant." Consequently, by the time SATs came around we were so uptight that if someone had touched us with a feather we'd have shattered like glass.

However, we pulled ourselves together for the final hurdles. She did the easy part: filled in the forms and wrote the essays, while we did the hard part: wrote the checks. That done we sat back grinning and telling everyone how easy it had been. Honest.

Until just the other day, when our second daughter came home grinning from ear to ear. "Set the alarm early tomorrow, Mum. It's PSATs."

Good grief, here we go again!

Chicago Daily News

News Lady column
On the Runway
by Brenda F. Smith

Flattery will get you into the most peculiar places.

For example, in my—comparative--youth, a Chicago business-man decided to invite local women's groups to send members to his shop to take part in a scheme that he hoped would give him new customers. For this he offered a modest sum to each of the groups in order to fund their charities.

My people had the oldest members. In fact, I, at forty-five or so was the youngest of them all. Other groups sent much younger women. "You are the only member of the group that can do it," fellow members of the group assured me. I could actually have been mother to the rest of them; I even heard one of them refer to me as Grandma.

The first morning we were introduced to the runway, and the clothes we'd be wearing. Mine was made of some black material and was so tight I had trouble taking even one step. It came with red shoes that pinched my toes and had eight-inch heels on which I was supposed to totter down the runway. I did so, my knees knocking like castanets.

When I first saw it, that aisle looked long enough for a 707 plane to take off.

Of course, before the show I had imagined the borders of the runway filled with newspaper journalists eager to describe our gorgeous clothes for their breathless readers, in the *Chicago Daily News,* or even the *New York Times*. On the day reality prevailed. Three or four local rags sent their most junior reporters to describe us to their readers, and this write-up appeared in four local papers in Illinois and Indiana that none of us had ever heard of.

The day came with me hoping that at least I wouldn't disgrace myself.

I managed to stay in my feet, but only just and was appalled when we were told to turn around and retrace our steps. If my dress had allowed me to fall, I'd have fainted on the spot. With as much cool as when the fridge is on the blink, I tottered down that huge expanse of carpet for the second time, hearing on each side sibilant female voices saying, "Poor old thing, she shouldn't have taken this on." By the time I had made my ungraceful exit at the other end of the runway, I was fully clothed but hardly in my right mind. For me, enough was enough.

However, the adventure taught me one useful lesson: that for someone of my advanced years, modeling is for the birds—the dolly birds, that is.

Chicago Daily News
News Lady column
Taking the Train
by Brenda F. Smith

"Taking the train?" They were astonished. "No one takes a train these days, they're dullsville."

I disagreed. "Nonsense! American trains may be old fashioned, but they're never dull."

I find there's nothing more likely to shut an American up than to tell him or her that something in his or her country is old fashioned—they just aren't used to it. So, after chuntering something like, "You're scared of flying, that's what!" they set off for their two-hour trip to the airport looking smug.

The fact that I am a little dubious about flying ("scared rigid," is how my husband puts it), has nothing to do with the way I feel about trains. If the wastes of desert and orange grove prove a little passé to members of the Now Generation who are used to flying in screaming jets and arriving in London or Los Angeles several hours ahead of their stomachs, but for those of us who remember wartime films, and songs such as "Chattanooga Choo Choo," they are a joy. From the moment I bought my ticket from a man with Trainman written in gold letters on his cap, I felt like Katie Hepburn off on an illicit forty-eight-hour pass.

The station, too, was from another era: a vast, echoing marble hall with fan vaulting and stained glass windows where red-capped porters trundled mountains of luggage to the waiting train (no weight limit here). And when it was time to leave, no impersonal, tinny voice squawked at us from the PA system, but guards came to the waiting rooms to tell us, "We loadin' the Capital," or "The Panama Limited," or, for me, "The California Zephyr." I really felt I was going places and that I'd get there in one piece. Meanwhile, overhead, our with-it jetsetters would be jouncing around in the air pockets, and serve them right.

The guards looked after us, serving good food on tables resplendent with tablecloths, good china, and glasses of wine. They even entertained us, singing and encouraging us to join in: "Day-o, Day-o. Daylight come and me wan' go home."

I thought we sounded pretty good.

And the scenery was spectacular, with the mountains, both east and west, the great Mississippi River, the deserts full of flowering cacti, fields smothered in the blue of poppies, and many introduced flowers on the roadsides, such as white daisies, blue lupines, tiger lilies.

Out on the tracks the train panted like some splendid silver beast, breathing steam from every pore, its searchlight piercing the darkness like some mad, Cyclopean eye. Later, when we reached the Rockies, two more diesels would be added to help haul us, slowly and majestically, over the Continental Divide, through the canyons and salt flats, the wastes of desert and orange groves down to the shore.

Taking the train had proved to be an adventure.

Chicago Daily News

News Lady column
Music Lovers at Play
by Brenda F. Smith

So Mike Royko, the famous *Chicago Daily News* columnist, suffers when the fellow in the next seat at the movies goes *Tsah*! Ha, what does he know of suffering?

For your deep-down, can't-stand-it-another-minute of suffering may I suggest he try the Symphony?

I speak with authority, having been a travelling concertgoer for many years. Which doesn't mean I travel from city to city, attending concerts now in Boston, now in New York. No, I travel only in Chicago's Symphony Hall. Every season I change my seat location, moving from the ground floor to the balcony, from the balcony to the gallery, in a desperate attempt to find a place where I'll be surrounded by people who like to listen to music.

Now you might suspect that Orchestra Hall would be the place to find such people, but not a bit of it. People go to Orchestra Hall for all kinds of reasons; listening to music isn't one of them.

Many a lady, for example, feels that she's a member of the orchestra, and while Sir Georg might think he's conducting a piece for violin and orchestra, what he's actually conducting is something for violin and orchestra—plus handbag accompaniment.

As the orchestra thunders along forte through the louder portions of the piece, I know I'm safe. It's when we reach the pianissimo parts that the trouble starts. First I feel my neighbor stiffen in her seat as she prepares to make her entrance. Quietly, she moves her instrument into her lap, then, just as the music enters its quietest, most lyric phase: SNAP, she opens her purse, CRACKLE, she unwraps her boiled candy, POP, she closes her purse. Cereal music, you might say. In between she rattles her charm bracelet.

Then there's the guy who thinks he's Sir Georg himself, but instead of conducting with a baton, he uses his head—half a beat behind the orchestra. Which is also true of the lady who plays the piano on the railing in front of her seat. Or the fellow who beats time with his foot on the wooden floor.

And if you thought that all the villains in the old west died out with the century, you're wrong. They are alive and well and living in Orchestra Hall, but instead of rustling cattle they're rustling programs.

If you add to all this activity the coughing, the humming, the fidgeting, the long, rumbling conversations, the coming-in-late and the going-out-early, it seems to me there's only one thing to be done: Sir Georg has to turn around and conduct the audience instead.

The Orchestra can listen to us for a change.

Chicago Daily News

News Lady column
The Empty Nest: Not so lonely, after all
by Brenda F. Smith

"Be ready for it," they said, shaking their heads gloomily. "When it happened to me I just fell apart. Why should you be any different?"

With enemies like those, I thought, who needs enemies?

Not that my friends were any help. "I just fell apart," they echoed mournfully. "You'll see."

So it was no wonder that, when we left our youngest child at college last fall, looking small, pathetic, and much too young, I fell apart.

I entered so whole-heartedly into my new role as Keeper of the Empty Nest, that old What's-His-Name-had to drive all the way home, while I busied myself with soggy handkerchiefs.

When we arrived home, there was no rock music blasting from the radio in the basement, or slamming of the refrigerator door, and it was then that I gradually began to realize that an empty nest might have a few things going for it.

Take that rock music. Now it was great to be able to loll back as the strains of my favorite Brahms concerto dripped into the room, knowing that no one was about to augment it with a touch of Dylan from the radio in the kitchen.

Then, too, it was surprising how light heartedly I mixed my evening martini, not having to defend my indulgence of what she labeled, "Mum's drug."

Or, when I lifted the phone in order to call a friend, I didn't hear someone on the extension yelling, "Mum, this is an *important* and *private* call!"

But the major joy, I think, was to be able to go to bed with my husband uninterrupted. Young marrieds may doubt that there is anything worse than having a four year old wander into the bedroom at a crucial moment. But teenagers wander in, too, and *they* know what's going on.

Yes, the youngest's first year away is over. I've missed my girls terribly. I even enjoyed their rock music, for a while. But when they go back to college this fall, I'll no doubt shed a tear or two, but this is one nest where the old bird will be keeping all her feathers.

Chicago Daily News
News Lady column
It's a Cat's Life
by Brenda F. Smith

There's a rumor going about that cats are good for us old folk, that they bring our blood pressure down, and make us smile at people we'd normally cut dead. Go get yourself a cat is the cry! You'll be healthier, you'll live longer, you'll be nicer to know. Don't believe a word of it.

I've had cats ever since my daughter's two arrived on my doorstep three years ago, and I know whereof I speak. Since then, I cry a lot, my blood pressure has soared to astronomical heights, and I'm a whole lot nastier than I used to be.

The first thing I learned about raising cats is that it's pretty much the same as raising children, only harder. Remember the day they had to have their shots? You spent the morning assuring them that it wouldn't hurt and the rest of it explaining why it did. They spent the afternoon complaining that you'd killed them.

It's the same with cats. When they sense you are about to take them to the vet they disappear, usually up the chimney. When you arrive at the surgery, impossibly late and covered in soot and cat hair, the receptionist will ask for their names. That's when you'll discover that although it's okay if you reply Lancelot or Euphemia, it's different if they are Rat and Toosh. "Is there an accent on Touché's name?" the receptionist will ask. There isn't, but she'll put one there anyway in order to give the surgery a bit more class. When you get the cats home, they'll go into a decline, running fevers and meowing piteously.

Also like children, cats often refuse food, even if they liked it last time. This is why you'll be left with a fridge full of opened cat food cans and very thin cats, rather in the way you are left with opened jars of peanut butter, thin children, and neighbors who threaten to report you to the authorities. Very occasionally your cats will gnaw daintily on the hindquarters of a rat, only to throw it up again when your back's turned. Usually on the rug. Children do the same with broccoli.

Cats also keep late hours. Believe me, if you've not waited up for a cat you haven't lived. By the time midnight comes around, you're convinced she's out with the randiest tom on the block, has been savaged by a slavering Doberman, flattened by the car driven by the drink-crazed boy next door, or all of the above. Exactly what you feared when your daughter's out after curfew.

You get the picture? Raising children (and cats) was well and good when we were twenty-five. Right? Now it's time to totter on to other things, without having to get up to let the cats in—or out. (Since there are two of them, for me it's in *and* out).

It's true that when talking to your cat—or even gerbil-owning neighbors—you have to listen to an awful lot of waffle about their pets before you can get a word in about your own. Which reminds me, I have a photo of Rat and Toosh somewhere.

Hey, wait, don't go! It'll only take a minute!

WESTWARD HO!

These are two poems I wrote while at Roosevelt.

Suicide
Was it glorious to die young,
To choose the time and place,
Not to know the dimming joy,
The gradual erosion of the dream?
What did you think of that mad March morning,
White clouds whipped and whirling,
The brown tarn swirling,
The young lamb's call?

Did you not recall the day we leaned,
Breathless on Helvelyn's cairn,
Drowsed by sunlight,
Drugged by windblown myrtles,
Deafened by skylarks?

But you pointed to the clouds above Griffell,
And you predicted,
Rain before nightfall.

Generation
She said to me, "I don't like being old,"
And hid her twisted hands beneath her shawl.
She was young once, and graceful, slim and tall,
Her laugh was eager and her brown eyes bold—
My children have her eyes. Now in the cold
Of Autumn afternoon, upon the wall
Our shadows, side by side, fall
Bleakly. Beyond the garden gate the old
Yew tree crouches, huddled from the blast.
We walk about the orchard, note how leafless are the branches,
Talk of last season's apples and how they can't compare
With this year's crop. My daughter dances past
Waving her plump young fingers in the air.

CHAPTER 32

America by Train

JOE AND I DID a lot of traveling with our children to England almost every summer before they went to college, and also to conferences and Joe's field trips during the academic year. I was okay in the car and on trains, but modern air travel reduces me to a billiard ball: easily pushed around. For me it usually begins at the check-in line, intensifies as I sit in one of those hard, plastic waiting-room chairs, and reaches a crescendo when I'm packed, elbow-to-elbow with three hundred others in a plane designed, it seems, for two hundred and fifty. It doesn't help when, although I would rather read than watch a movie, my neighbors mutter and give me indignant looks if I dare to turn on my light. This was why we decided to take the Southwest Chief train to Albuquerque for one of Joe's scientific conferences.

I knew we were onto something different when we entered the waiting room in the Chicago station for the trip west, and found that it had marble floors, pictures on the walls, and was crowded with people sitting at ease in large, overstuffed chairs— real people sitting in real chairs. Instead of a gaggle of middle-aged men with suits, identical haircuts, and laptop computers, there were a couple of Wisconsin farmers in caps, gnarled fingers at unaccustomed rest on the arms of their chairs, as they swapped yarns about their herds or their corn. Two grandmothers showed off pictures of their grandkids; children ran excitedly about; an itinerant preacher in a "Jesus Saves" sweatshirt handed out tracts, while a young American Indian, a bandanna about his head, talked proudly about his reservation to a couple of jean-clad students. For me this was a real slice of America.

It was the same on the train: the sleeping-car attendants' smiles were friendly when we appeared, real smiles that came from men and women whose feet probably hurt toward the end of the day. Being real people, they treated us like real people, too. On a plane, if you should inadvertently press the call button when groping in vain for the light switch, the attendant will come, smiling her plastic smile, her voice as sweet as though addressing a not-too-bright kindergartener, to point out your error. On the train, when I asked the trainman for a second time how to get to the dining car, he replied, with a sigh of exasperation, "Ma'am, I done told you that already." I liked that.

Reality reigned also in the dining car. There we were served, not with plastic food on a plastic tray to be eaten with a plastic knife and fork, but with real food eaten from real plates using real cutlery, served on a real table covered with a real linen cloth. And when I hesitated to order one of the over-rich desserts, the waiter gave me a nudge and said, "Go on, order it. It'll do you good." Toward the end of the meal, the wait staff got together to sing us a chorus of "Day-O," and we all joined in with "Daylight come and I wanna go home." When has that ever happened on American, or British Airlines?

Moreover, how often have air travelers looked out of their window, as we looked out from our dome car, to see a coyote howling beside the track, or a cowboy herding his cattle in the evening light, or a group of pronghorns scrambling away as the train whistle echoed mournfully over the high plains? From thirty thousand feet, it's unlikely they would see the red splashes of Indian paintbrush, or the wash of blue lupines among the hills as we did. Yes, you can look through the windows of a plane and be thrilled by the clouds seen from above, by the landscape below you stretched out like a map. But a map isn't scenery, only a facsimile of the real thing.

For me, plane travel, which used to be fun, has become what is most wrong with modern life. It separates us from reality and from one another. Computers do it, too, as do the Internet, e-mail, and the gaggle of social media where we pretend to talk to one another, all the while putting out a totally false picture of who we are and what we are about. We watch Netflix either alone or with a family member. We are used to our family's sense of humor, but when in a cinema, full of strangers who laugh when we do, we get the feeling that the whole world could be kin, if only we tried a little harder.

Admittedly, train travel has its drawbacks—Kansas is one of them—but I'm beginning to think that the pious lady in the old joke got it right: "If the Good Lord had meant us to fly," she declared, "he wouldn't have given us the railways."

CHAPTER 33

Working Again

WHEN I FIRST ARRIVED in America in 1951, I found work in the false-tooth factory, and then as a receptionist at the "Gee Whiz" Laboratory where Joe worked. For the next fifteen years, I raised the girls, and volunteered at the University of Chicago children's hospital, as well as serving as president of Hyde Park Co-op Homes for several years. And then I found the job that I truly loved.

After graduating from Roosevelt University, I began working as studio manager for a charity called Recording for the Blind. RFB had been founded by a woman named Anne MacDonald who, while working for the Women's Auxiliary of the New York Public Library, received many letters from GIs returning blinded from the Second World War. Under the GI Bill, returning soldiers were offered free tuition at universities all over the country. Blinded students were unable to take up the offer, until in 1952, Mrs. McDonald established what she named a "recovery studio" in New York, which she called Recording for the Blind, or RFB, with herself as president. Afterward, she encouraged friends to open offices in other towns, including Chicago, Phoenix, Oak Ridge, Tennessee, and Athens, Georgia. Today, RFB has studios all over the country. In the 1970s, the company also began reading for dyslexic students, and is now referred to as RFB&D.

In the 1970s, we used reel-to-reel and later cassette tapes, followed by CDs. We read textbooks and literary works for students from their earliest school years through their PhD degree and beyond. My job was to manage the branch studio, housed in the basement of the new Geophysical Sciences Department at the University of Chicago, where Joe had his office on the third floor.

I, and an assistant, recruited and trained volunteers until they were able to pass a reading exam in their subject. We also trained volunteers to act as "monitors," in which they operated the recording machines and listened to the readers in order to detect and correct any mistakes they made, such as mispronunciations or misreading of the texts, graphs, and charts. I also dealt with borrowers and their requests, and helped record many of the books myself. My children and grandchildren will find this unbelievable, but I passed a test that allowed me to read, not only literature, but also computer texts; computer language was less complicated back then.

To recruit volunteers, I relied on word-of-mouth, advertisements in the student newspaper, and a yearly countrywide Record-a-thon, during which we supplied coffee and snacks to hungry students and other potential volunteers as an introduction to the studio. The work was interesting, and during the years I was with RFB&D I met many talented people among the volunteers: students, faculty, and members of the local community, including the novelist Sara Paretsky, author of the Chicago-based V. I. Warshawski mystery series, who came to the studio to read one of her mysteries. Mysteries are not often assigned for study, but having an author read her work in our studio was a form of advertisement for both RFB&D and Ms. Paretsky. Because the work involved books, it was my kind of work.

During the years I worked for RFB&D, I had several coworkers, among them Ria Ahlstrom, who took care of the studio two days a week, and several student helpers, one of whom later married a school friend of Sue's. After I retired, I volunteered as a reader at the downtown studio in Chicago, and later at the one in Cambridge, Massachusetts, when I moved to Brookline.

CHAPTER 34

Geophysicist at Work

Joseph V. Smith

AT THE UNIVERSITY OF Chicago, Joe was engrossed in his teaching and research in x-ray crystallography, geology, and geophysics. I loved the unexpected beauty of the crystal models Joe constructed from plastic rods, the thin slices of rock he cut and polished for his work in the Lab, the huge, toothed chunks of rose quartz in his display cabinets. He showed them to me as though they were the center of the universe, as they were, to him. He explained how each mineral in a rock had its own crystalline structure and was an entity in itself, with characteristic planes and angles, its atoms and molecules arranged in predictable, geometric patterns. He spoke of symmetry, glide planes, of space groups, of the interlocking of one crystal

211

of a substance with its neighbor. He showed me his crystals under an electron microscope: gold-like threads of chalcopyrite; sage-green needles of dioptase; honey-yellow wulfenite; bloodred cinnabar. He was always serious as he pondered a problem, and when everything began to fall into place, he would cry, "Elegant!'

Joe began his scientific career with many disadvantages, although he would view them as opportunities to construct exactly what he needed. Lacking the machines with which to do his work, he had to build an x-ray generator from scratch at the Carnegie Geophysical Laboratory in Washington, complete his early crystallographic work with the now obsolete system of cards called Beevers-Lipson strips, and struggle with a computer that consisted of an entire roomful of machinery. He later became expert in using up-to-date computers, modern x-ray equipment, and the synchrotrons at Argonne and Brookhaven National Laboratories. Eventually he became a consultant for both of those organizations. During the eighties and nineties, he also advanced the use of the electron microscope and the ion microprobe to get chemical analyses of mineral fragments, and continued to be involved in NASA's lunar program. As a consultant for Union Carbide, working with Edith Flanagan, he pioneered the use of zeolites as molecular sieves, which led to the removal of lead from gasoline and to phosphate-free detergents.

Over his career, he wrote over four hundred scientific papers, including many on feldspars, for scientific journals

including *Science, Scientific American, American Mineralogist, Journal of Geology, Journal of Physical Chemistry,* and *Nature.* Our friend William (Mac) MacKenzie had introduced him to the mineral during our stay in Washington; Joe ultimately became the world's expert on feldspars, producing throughout his career two volumes, the first, *Feldspar Minerals: Crystal Structure and Physical Properties,* and the second, *Feldspar Minerals: Chemical and Textural Properties,* both published by Springer Verlag in 1974. He published a revised edition of his first volume with Prof. William L. Brown from Centre National de la Recherche Scientifique in Vandoeuvre-les-Nancy in northeastern France. In 1982, his *Geometrical and Structural Crystallography* was published by Wiley. He also collaborated with Prof. Barry Dawson, from St. Andrews and later Edinburgh University, in work on the volcanic rocks of Kenya. Much later, Joe organized a conference on the threat to the earth of asteroid and comet impacts, earth-quakes, and volcanic activity, and because he believed that human activity was damaging the earth, the problem of climate change.

In the 1970s and 1980s, Joe became internationally known for his scientific work, and won several awards, among them the Murchison Medal of the Geological Society (London) in 1980, and in 1982 the Roebling Medal, the highest award of the Mineralogical Society of America; in the latter case, he was then the youngest person to win this honor.

He was elected to both Britain's Royal Society in 1978 and the (US) National Academy of Sciences in 1986 and was called upon to lecture in many parts of the world. Many who knew Joe have told me he was a brilliant scientist and produced much original work; Joe would have thought that "brilliant" was overdoing things. He used to say that he got where he was, not by brilliance, but by perseverance and hard work, which he had learned from his boyhood on a farm, where he helped his father milk by hand a herd of cows twice a day, and plough using a horse. His favorite motto, repeated ad nauseam to the family, was "Organization is the key to success." When a theory Joe pioneered was added to by some up-and-coming young scientist, he was pleased; science, he told me, was always being modified by new minds and new scientific equipment and methods.

In the nineties he raised huge sums for the development of Argonne's Center for Advanced Radiation Sources. CARS had offices at the University of Chicago and Joe was head of it for several years.

As CARS wrote in a tribute to Joe:

Joseph Smith developed a far-reaching, deeply ambitious vision to place the University of Chicago at the forefront of synchrotron X-ray science. With characteristic determination, political acumen, and farsightedness, Joe pursued this plan in the face of vocal skepticism from many quarters.

Never one to think small, Joe realized that such a project required some unconventional tactics. With his usual enthusiasm, he sought out broad support beyond the University; Representation across disciplines (sectors proposed for biology, geology, chemistry, and soil/environmental science); Involvement with industrial research; and Collaboration with the nascent synchrotron community in Australia.

While such strategies are now commonplace in large-scale science, in 1989 they were still considered somewhat heretical. However, time proved Joe right on nearly all counts. The Center for Advanced Radiation Sources now operates four sectors—just as Joe originally envisioned.

Perhaps because Joe had daughters and no sons, perhaps because he was offended by anyone who tried to limit someone else's advancement, due to his early experience working with a brilliant female scientist, Helen Megaw, at the Cavendish Laboratory in

Cambridge, he was appalled by the small number of female scientists, and mounted a campaign in the Geophysics Department at the University of Chicago to hire more women scientists as professors.

During the 1990s, he was put in charge of hiring a number of new faculty members for the department. He spoke with scientists around the world, and scoured the research and writings of women scientists to discover those doing the most important work. He brought the female candidates to the university, where he and some of his colleagues put on their best show. I must say that he had results: a number of the women scientists whom he had recruited were offered positions, and some of them accepted, greatly increasing the number of women in the department. Although some of the men in the department were less than enthusiastic about Joe's work to bring in talented women scientists, Joe considered his work promoting female scientists to be among the best things he'd ever done.

Joe, ever the scientist, included scientific thought in his approach to his health: keeping up-to-date by reading scientific articles that recommended various vitamins and minerals. These included anything containing vitamin C, along with zinc pills. I expect the vitamin C did him good; I was never sure about the zinc, although it seemed to do him no harm. Whatever the cause, Joe produced original scientific work almost to the end of his life.

CHAPTER 35

Beverly Shores, Indiana

IN 1974, WE FOUND ourselves with two houses: one in Chicago, one in Indiana. Our friends from the University of Chicago, the Goldsmiths, the Fultzes, and the Kleppas had weekend homes in the Indiana Dunes area and often invited us to visit. Eventually, we began to feel it might be time to look for a place of our own.

It was not long before we found a possible candidate in a small village named Beverly Shores in the Indiana Dunes National Lakeshore, which overlooked Lake Michigan. Possible, that is, until we were told its price: $115,000. Joe was earning a good salary at that stage, to which I added my pittance of $28,000 a year from Recording for the Blind; nevertheless in the seventies, $115,000 appeared to us a staggering sum. After much thought, discussion, and a great deal of pacing up and down the beach, Joe decided we could offer the owner $110,000. To our surprise, he accepted, and we found ourselves the proud owners of the house we named Ballantrae after my parents' home in Derbyshire.

It was a handsome house, built into a dune, redbrick at the basement level and cedar siding for the main floor. The basement had a large sitting room, another large room that Joe used as his office, a bathroom, and a laundry room. The windows of the two large rooms of the basement, and those on the main floor, looked onto a garden consisting of a small lawn with beds of roses and other flowers; beyond was an established dune.

On the main floor of Ballantrae House were a large living room and kitchen, two bedrooms facing south toward the dune, a family bathroom, and a master bedroom that overlooked the lake and had its own bathroom. The hallway on the main floor proved to be the perfect place for the collection of etchings, lithographs, woodcuts, and paintings Joe and I had begun accumulating. There was artwork in nearly every room of the house.

The windows of the living room and kitchen on the main floor had magnificent views over the lake. On that first January I wrote, "the trees are ice covered, and the lake has eaten away much of the ice shelf that formed last week. A blizzard is blowing and the lake has breakers to the horizon. There are many gulls flying along the shore, but no other birds are stirring." It was a brutal winter, and in February the cold reached the lowest temperature ever recorded in that part of the world: minus seventeen degrees Fahrenheit. The roads were clogged with eighty inches of snow.

By March the winter was loosening its grip, the juncos (also called snowbirds) were beginning to gather for their migration north to Canada, from which they would return in October, and the crows, chickadees, myrtle warblers, and robins were active. Meanwhile leaves were thickening on the dogwoods, lilacs, and redbud trees. By April we could hear the chirp of red-winged blackbirds staking out their claims among the reeds of the marsh on the other side of the dunes, along with swamp egrets and an occasional heron. On the lake in addition to gulls, there were geese, mergansers, and black coots.

The view from Joe's office window, overlooking the dune behind the house, was rich with weeds and wild flowers both spring and summer, among them the brilliant blue of hepatica, along with *Gaillardia*, violets, mayapples, drifts of purple lupines, columbines, honesty, lilies of the valley, and that curse of American woodlands, poison ivy. Beyond the dune, on our bicycle trips along the path through the marsh, we found the verges golden with marsh marigolds, alongside skunk cabbages, teasels, and various marsh grasses. Later in the summer, we gathered jars full of blackberries, which we took home to freeze or make into jam.

Lake Michigan was often stormy with enormous waves, gulls swooping over their white crests. We saw the occasional ore boat creeping down from the north, carrying iron ore from Duluth to the steel mills of Gary. On foggy days we sometimes saw a mirage to the west in which Chicago's Sears Tower and other skyscrapers appeared to float above the surface of the lake like ghosts. We often had brilliant sunsets; those I particularly remember were in early spring, when a serene sky glowed like gold through the black pencil marks that were the trunks and branches of trees not yet in leaf. On clear nights the sky looked like black velvet, stars scattered upon it like jewels; the kind of display that is killed by streetlights and never appeared above our home in Chicago. Ballantrae House proved to be a beautiful and deeply satisfying home.

The road where our house stood continued as far northeast as Michigan City, but after a pier was built out into the lake, near Mount Baldy—a large dune just outside town—the road for several hundred yards was washed away. The new pier had strengthened the north-south movement of the waves on that stretch of the coast so that the water began to erode the beaches and the road between Michigan City and Gary. Because of this, shortly after we moved to Indiana, I watched two houses on the lakeshore float away into the waves. The owners, fortunately, got out in time.

For a while after we bought Ballantrae House, we hung on to our house in Hyde Park, driving into town every Monday morning and back to the country every Friday night. But we frugal Limeys, remembering the austerity of the Great Depression and the war years, soon felt that owning two houses was overdoing things, so that when our next-door neighbors at Co-op Homes asked if we'd consider selling them our Hyde Park house so they could add it to theirs, we agreed. But we still needed a *pied-à-terre* in Chicago, and for a while lived during the week at the university's Quadrangle Club; we later bought a one-bedroom apartment at Vista Homes on Stony Island Avenue on the Midway, but spent most of our time in our lovely new home in Beverly Shores.

CHAPTER 36

Home in America

BY THE MID-SEVENTIES, CHICAGO was beginning to seem more like home, at least one of my homes, because now I felt that I had two: one in England where I grew up and my mother, sister, two brothers, aunts, uncles, and cousins lived, and one in America, where I split my time between Hyde Park and Beverly Shores.

The girls, of course, were beginning their own lives as adults. Ginnie graduated from college in 1975, with a degree in English literature, and went to work at Pergamon Press, Oxford, where she house-sat for John Wain, the Oxford Professor of Poetry for the summer. At Pergamon, women, even those with excellent college degrees like Ginnie, were only allowed to work typing up the journals, whereas men with the same degree were hired as editors. After her summer in Oxford, Ginnie moved back to Hyde Park, and worked as a production assistant at the University of Chicago Press. Weekends were often spent with us at our new house in Beverly Shores.

Sue attended Oberlin College for a year, and then took time out to work and travel. She moved to Minneapolis where she worked at a co-op bakery and grocery store, and at an elementary school as a teaching assistant in a special-education class. In the summer of 1975, she traveled to visit Ginnie in Oxford, England, then traveled overland to India, passing through France, Italy, Greece, Turkey, Iran, Afghanistan, and Pakistan. In India, she became very ill, and we were making plans to fly there to bring her back when she wrote that she was on her way home. She spent the following year beginning to heal in both mind and body, realizing that the peace she had sought in eastern lands and practices was illusory. She said it took a trip around the world for her to come home. Since that time, she has lived out her faith as a committed Christian.

Over the years, I had grown fond of Hyde Park. It had changed a great deal since we first drove into its dark, satanic streets in 1960, especially after the two power station chimneys across the Midway were dismantled and the last of the stock-yards to the west of the city closed their doors. As a result, the air was breathable: less redolent of coal dust and cattle, and the violence of the streets had somewhat abated. The university had also begun putting up handsome new buildings. One was the Henry Hinds Laboratory for Geophysical Sciences, where Joe had his Lab and RFB&D their quarters. At the same time the town planted trees along the Midway to replace its dying elms, while the university created new gardens, renovated old ones, and tidied up the quadrangles. In 2009, the university appropri-ated a statue of the Swedish botanist, Carl Linnaeus, who in the 1730s developed a method of naming and categorizing all life forms that is still used today. The statue had been on the north side of the city, and was now installed on the Midway close to the house of the president. All this activity made for an increasingly handsome campus.

We enjoyed our walks in the neighborhood: along the Midway east to the Japanese garden on Wooded Island; to Promontory Point on the lakefront, with its bicycle path that follows the shore of Lake Michigan to the city center and beyond. Occasionally, we headed toward the west side of the Midway, where we watched Indian students playing cricket.

As if to prove that the new Hyde Park still had its problems, we came home one day to find that we had been burgled yet again. The person who did the deed must have noticed that Joe and I spent most weekends out of town and had pounced. I can't remember everything he took this time, except that my replacement engagement ring had disappeared. My first one had been lifted in a prior robbery.

Meanwhile, at Ballantrae House, Joe planted a vegetable garden alongside the driveway, and together we planted herbs, tomatoes, peppers, carrots, peas, and runner beans. Susan helped by planting seeds in the garden. By that time, alewives had invaded the Great Lakes and had seasonal die-offs when the beaches became littered with their corpses. Remembering the history of the local Indian tribes, Sue gathered up some of the fishy bodies to bury in little mounds of soil along with her pumpkin seeds. A good idea, but unfortunately the groundhogs thought so too, and dug them up again.

Eventually, those animals proved to be a problem when they attacked much of our crop. To counter them, Joe bought a cage-like trap, lured them into it with various foods, put the trap in the car and drove to the nearby State Park where he set them free. He later became convinced that on his voyages out he must have passed someone en route to Beverly Shores on a similar mission, because the next morning we invariably found groundhogs once more making themselves at home among our vegetables. On one occasion, we captured six of them at once and Joe hauled them even further into the State Park. These animals, along with chipmunks, were also fond of our raspberries, which ripened later in the summer; it became a constant fight to get to the fruit first.

In addition to groundhogs and chipmunks, we discovered the Indiana fauna to include deer, muskrats, several kinds of squirrel (including the flying kind), rabbits, and red foxes. In the coldest weather, squirrels sometimes appeared outside the glass doors of our deck "with their paws raised in supplication." A bit of sentimentality on my part, but they did hang about until we gave them food. On one dreadful occasion, one of them fell down the chimney and landed in the fire, which set its tail ablaze. Joe managed to douse the flames, get it into a bucket and outside, where it died. After that, we blocked the entrance to the chimney with a grill so that animals or birds searching for warmth were no longer able to creep inside.

Among our feathered visitors were snowy owls, blue jays, mourning doves, and bank swallows that built their nests in holes they made in a wall of sand overlooking the beach. In the marsh we often spotted herons, and hovering over or on the lake were hawks, cormorants, loons, and Canada geese. Sandpipers ran busily up and down the shore, and as the year progressed we saw red-winged blackbirds, orioles, and evening grosbeaks. A bird-feeder that Joe attached to a fir tree on the dune behind us became the stopping-off point for many a hungry bird. Meanwhile, among all this twitter, frogs in the nearby marsh twanged like rubber bands—until we walked by and they fell silent. We had plenty of company in Beverly Shores.

CHAPTER 37

In Which I Become an American, and We Think Again of England

SHORTLY AFTER WE MOVED into Ballantrae House, Joe finally persuaded me that it was time I became an American citizen. He had taken the oath some years before, but although I was fond of America (apart from loathing the trigger-happy part), I still felt British and continued to fight the idea. However, after a Swedish friend warned me that the girls, as children of a foreign national, would have to pay much higher taxes on any money they might inherit from me, I decided for this not very praiseworthy reason to become an American citizen.

Taking a deep breath, I went to Valparaiso to join a large group of excited noncitizens to take the oath. I was almost too late for the ceremony, since I had been unaware that Valparaiso was in a different time zone from ours on Lake Michigan's southeast coast (who knew one state had two different time zones?) We motley crew—mostly Poles and Mexicans plus two Brits—took the pledge en masse, some of us, though not I, weeping the while.

The hall where the ceremony was held was magnificent and the man in charge made a gracious speech welcoming us. The ceremonial guard consisted of ten men: some short, some tall, some fat, some thin, some in-between; a group not at all guard-like. But the deed was done and, like a few other nationalities, I wouldn't lose my British citizenship as long as I didn't attempt to vote in Britain. I know that's unfair to people from some other countries whose governments won't tolerate dual citizenship, but I don't intend to write to my Member of Parliament about it. (I should add that the American law that said the heirs of foreigners would be more heavily taxed than the natives, no longer applies.)

⁓

In June 1977, Sir Brian Pippard, the head of the Cavendish Laboratory in Cambridge, England, contacted Joe out of the blue. He asked Joe to join the Cavendish as his second-in-command, in the newly created position of "Head of Department,"—a tremendous opportunity for Joe, and a wonderful homecoming for me.

In early July, Joe and Ginnie went home to Cambridge to look at housing for our move. Ginnie had just ended a job at the University of Chicago Press, where again opportunities for bright, ambitious women were stymied. In Cambridge, she met with the publisher of Cambridge University Press. He offered her a job with Sir Joseph Needham, a member of Gonville and Caius, Joe's old College. Sir Joseph was an expert in the history of Chinese science and the author of the series entitled *Science and Civilization in China.* He needed a personal assistant. Ginnie was thrilled with the job offer and was ready to move.

However, our daughter Susan had spent a difficult year in India, and had arrived home the previous year in poor health. Joe and I felt that our move to England might harm her full recovery, and after a lot of thought, we decided the risks were too great.

To turn down the offer of this position at the Cavendish was a hard decision to make. It was a troubling time for us, and Joe and I spent several months mulling over our options; should we, shouldn't we? Even after Joe had made the final decision that we stay in America, a decision in which I concurred, I still felt troubled about our chosen path. I knew Frost was right, and that "I shall be telling this with a sigh / Somewhere ages and ages hence: / Two roads diverged in a wood, and I— / I took the one less traveled by, / And that has made all the difference." Indeed it has.

For a long time, I was not sure that our decision was the correct one. Joe, of course, was more sensible: the choice was made; let's get on with it. Sometimes it pays to have a farmer's boy on board.

CHAPTER 38

Dragooning Our Visitors, and Joe's "Bathtub Float"

WHEN HE WASN'T BUSY in his office writing up his week's findings in the Lab, Joe was occupied with the garden: digging new beds, thinning out bushes, and constructing a brick path around the house to prevent the vulnerable dune from wearing away. Guests were not spared from these activities, and friends from as far away as Edinburgh in Scotland and Liege in France found themselves weeding our rose beds, or wheeling barrows full of bricks to help make the path. That path later became the target of a muskrat that built tunnels beneath it, dislodging the bricks that had been placed at the expense of much sweat.

The local flora of the Indiana Dunes, spring through fall, was a delight. It included wood anemones, phlox, May blobs, violets, and cranesbill, and among the early unfurling leaves, blossoming dogwood and redbud added their perfume. The dunes behind us were a sea of color through the year, not only from the various flowers that graced them, but from the leafy blaze of sassafras, oaks, maples, and sumacs that surrounded us in the fall. After the leaves had fallen, the ground was golden and brown with them.

In winter, too, the views were spectacular: the lake stilled by pancakes of ice and sometimes frozen from coast to coast;

the snow that cushioned the roads also thickened the outlines of trees along the lakefront. One day, we arrived to find our house completely snowed in. It took almost a day for us to dig out a path to the garage in minus-twenty-five-degree temperatures. The wind chill factor that day was minus eighty degrees Fahrenheit. Milder January days tended to be what I once described as "gray and mizzling, the hooter at the lakefront blasting its warning of thick fog." (According to my 1981–82 notebooks, England, too, experienced much colder temperatures that winter: minus seven degrees in one case. Later there were floods during which Tewkesbury was surrounded by water, and part of York evacuated.)

As in Chicago, we entertained a great deal, often inviting both faculty and students to visit for a day at the beach; several times we took students on field trips along the lakeshore.

We spent one weekend at Devil's Lake in southern Wisconsin, where we camped overnight, and the next day climbed the steep path to the top of the cliffs, Joe and the students examining the Baraboo quartzite and the glacial history of the area.

At Thanksgiving and Christmas, we often had as many as thirty guests, students and faculty, around two tables. After dinner on those occasions, the younger children of our guests shrieked with delight when Joe slipped a record onto the turntable, and it was time for them to follow him in a march about the house, accompanied by the Scottish ditty—"A Hundred Pipers." It was the same tune Joe and the girls marched to when they were young.

Ginnie and Sue would often come for Thanksgiving, and always spend Christmas with us in Beverly Shores. Ginnie had begun her two years gaining an MBA from Harvard University, after which she moved to Manhattan to work in book publishing. Sue had transferred from Oberlin to the University of Wisconsin–Madison and majored in art history. Having learned drafting at the graphics department at the University of Chicago, and helping Joe with drawings for his book, *Geometrical and Structural Crystallography*, published in 1982, she found a part-time job at the Department of Geology and Geophysics in Madison as an illustrator, while working on her BA and later a master's degree in library science and children's literature. To cover her bases, she became certified as a school librarian.

I was delighted to be invited to join a book group in Beverly Shores where the leader, a professor of English literature at the University of Chicago, drove out every week to meet us in Beverly Shores' Town Hall. Later, a friend, Kay Franklin, invited Joe and me to join a play-reading group, made up of people from the town and nearby communities who met once a month. Joe made a name for himself in the role of Estragon in Samuel Beckett's *Waiting for Godot*. For the part, he wore his boots, gardening trousers, and a jacket in less-than-pristine condition. Sometimes, coming to the club from a session in the garden, he wore similar garb, until one woman asked him if he was disguised as a scarecrow for Halloween. Fashion was never Joe's strong point.

Beverly Shores had a local newspaper, the "News Letter," with Kay as editor, and it was not long before she recruited me to help. The paper came out once a month and was full of local news sent in by members of the town council, the various book and play-reading groups, and with stories, or articles on the local flora and fauna, contributed by readers. My reporting was not free of gaffes: One week, on hearing strange sounds from a nearby marsh, I reported that the geese had returned. Unfortunately, the geese turned out to be a chorus of frogs. On publishing weekends, a group gathered to put the paper together and find a suitable cover. It was not long before Kay decided she'd had enough, and so I was left holding the baby, a job I came to enjoy a great deal. I wrote an article on local happenings every month, and also one on gardening, local animals and plants, and sometimes descriptions of trips Joe and I had made to various parts of the country. When I had space to fill, Joe obliged by writing about the geology and nature of the area.

About that time, I was hired by the *American Journal of Sociology* to edit their journal every month, and became involved with the ABSR (the Association of Beverly Shores' Residents), as liaison with the Park Service. Joe was adviser to them on the erosion of the lakefront. We also joined efforts by the Park Service to protect the shores with sandbags, another chore for which we recruited anyone unfortunate enough to be our guest at the time, including friend Barry Dawson from Edinburgh, our daughter Virginia, and Joe's brother Tom when he visited us from Canada for Thanksgiving.

In 1982, Joe went to visit Clare Leighton, an artist living in Woodbury, Connecticut whose etchings we admired. Virginia, who was soon to graduate from Harvard Business School, accompanied him on that occasion. I later met the artist, and found her an interesting though egotistical woman, with the profile of an Indian on the nickel coin, and dyed red pigtails. We bought quite a few prints from her, including the Wedgwood set, which now graces the walls of Ginnie's living room. They were called Wedgwood because their pattern was used on actual plates made by the famous ceramic company.

Sometime during the eighties, I was asked to appear on a Chicago television program called *The Daybreak Show.* I have no memory of the occasion, or even of the show, but according to my notes, someone called Judy Maher interviewed me. I described her as being, "full of false bonhomie and plastered with pancake make-up." A friend assured me I did okay as a TV interviewee, but for some reason I never saw the tape. I wonder now if I was interviewed about my work with Recording for the Blind, which I had begun in the late seventies.

Close to Beverly Shores, we enjoyed visiting two historic sites with the girls. One, the Bailly Homestead, was established in 1822 by one of the first fur traders to the area, Joseph Bailly de Messein, who eventually farmed two thousand acres of land. After Bailly's death, Francis Howe, his son-in-law, took over the farm and began selling wood from the property for use in the building of a local railroad. Another son-in-law later brought in Swedish immigrants from Chicago to operate a sawmill on the premises.

Nearby was the Chellberg Farm, the home of early Swedish settlers who were among the first European arrivals in Northern

Indiana. The family purchased forty acres and in 1863 built their first, wooden, home on a glacial moraine. A year later, after the house burned down, they replaced it with a handsome brick house and began farming. Descendants of the Chellberg family owned and worked the farm until 1962 when it became a National Historic Landmark.

At one point in the eighties, we indulged in a rowboat that we kept anchored to a rock on the nearby beach, and when the evening was calm we rowed ourselves up the coast almost as far as Michigan City, or down to the Red Lantern, a pub and café that used to sit close to the beach in Beverly Shores. One day, after a northwest wind had roared through, churning the water into enormous waves, Joe went to check on the boat and found it gone. He had three theories: the boat was buried under sand that had drifted our way from further north; it had sailed away across the lake, maybe as far as Chicago, or it had been stolen. The truth was much more mundane: we discovered that the rock to which we'd anchored it had shifted down the beach during the storm and the rope used to tie it had broken. The next day a friend called to tell us he had discovered our boat, which had come ashore two miles down the coast. We shouldered the oars, walked down the beach to retrieve it, and after Joe rowed it and me back, tethered it more tightly to the rocks, this time with a chain.

Rowing was not our only form of exercise. We walked for miles around Beverly Shores and did a lot of cycling, often along the lakefront as far as the state park, returning along the bike path where we enjoyed a golden carpet of marsh mallows in the spring; in July, brown-eyed Susans, Queen Anne's lace, and irises. In the summer we also swam a great deal in the lake, while during fall through spring I joined my Hyde Park friends at the U of C's Ida Noyes pool. Joe's swimming style was the subject of family mirth. He would lie on his back, his torso a curve below the water, feet above kicking vigorously, his arms splashing frantically backward. He called it "the bathtub float." He also joined a group of bell ringers at a church in Hyde Park, where his arms and shoulders were given a more thorough workout. With Susan's help I also attempted to take up cross-country skiing on the marsh behind Ballantrae House, but ended up ludicrously sailing backward down any slight rise I encountered. That adventure didn't last long.

CHAPTER 39

Down Under

AUSTRALIA HAS ALWAYS BEEN my first choice of a foreign land. My love for this country, nicknamed "Down Under," or "Oz," began over fifty years earlier when, as a child of four or five, my father assured me that if I dug down far enough through English soil I would end up in Australia. Dad was probably trying to keep me busy for the afternoon, but it was not long before his garden, his pride and joy, began to look as though it had been invaded by a pack of koalas, as I, shoveling soil right and left, fancied that I already heard the grunt of wallaby and kangaroo.

In school, the map of Australia was an easy one for a child to remember. It was the country that resembled a lion, with Perth at the mouth, Darwin up around the ears, and Sydney and Melbourne at the back of the neck. New Zealand, on the other hand, was a bunch of islands that I kept confusing with Japan.

For homework, I drew magnificent maps of my beloved new land and, using all the crayons in the box, carefully put in gold and silver, cattle and sheep, pineapples and wheat, plus all those wonderful names: Whyalla, Wagga Wagga, and Wollongong. The teacher gave me a gold star; I was inescapably hooked.

In 1990, when Joe was asked to give a series of lectures in Australia with an itinerary that would take him to Sydney, Canberra, and Melbourne, on the east, Adelaide on the southeast coast, and finally Perth in Western Australia, without hesitation I told him I'd be accompanying him.

Our adventure began with a long flight from Chicago to Hawaii, where a stopover gave us time to have a look around the Big Island. The weather was mostly hot and humid although it became cooler the higher we climbed. We hired a car and drove to an area where the Mauna Loa volcano was spouting, its molten lava plunging down into a turquoise sea; a glorious scene. After this, we flew to Sydney, on Australia's east coast, where a man from the university's geology department met us and drove us to a small rental flat in a suburb where we were to stay. The flat was sparse, but adequate, and the suburb itself was in what appeared to be a rich businessman's haven. At first, we had no car, and it was necessary to catch a ferry every day to go into the city. To get to the dock we walked down a winding footpath, passing several very large houses among the trees. Our fellow commuters, also walking toward the ferry, looked most un-Australian, the men in well-pressed suits, one or two even sporting a bowler hat.

The ferry ride took about twenty minutes, passing on the south side of the bay the Royal Botanic Garden, and on the north the soaring Sydney Harbor Bridge. Utzon's famous opera house with its white wings, now a little discolored, sits in the center of the bay. Joe and I often stopped to drink coffee at an ocean-side café in order to admire the view over the harbor, and the palm and fig trees of the Royal Gardens that gave us our first sight of the kookaburra, colorful birds that laughed at us maniacally. We also watched ocean-going ships creeping in from the Tasman Sea to the port at Sydney Harbor. Behind our table, in an arc of gray stone, sat a row of small, attached buildings, which, when Sydney was a penal colony, had housed some of the first men to be exiled to this continent. These were criminals from the British Isles, few of them convicted of serious crimes, but for something minor, such as stealing a sheep.

Canberra is the home of Australia's parliament, and Sydney had a distinctly London-like bustle; however, during our first evening in Melbourne, our hostess told us: "This town's not like Sydney, you know. It was settled by *genuine* immigrants." She was not the only Melbourne native to set me straight. Only about 20 percent of Australians have a prisoner among their ancestors, and our hostess had no need to worry: I already had a good feeling about the town.

This was because in England after the war, when we were even hungrier than we had been during hostilities, Melbourne's library employees sent food parcels to those of us working in the County Libraries of Derbyshire. They probably chose us to receive their gifts because the Australian Melbourne had been named for a town in Derbyshire. I'll never forget the can of peaches that became mine after we received the parcel of goodies for which we drew lots. When I brought the tin home, it made me heroine of the day. In addition to peaches, the parcel contained chocolate, white flour, sugar, and lard, but because we hadn't seen tinned fruit for over five years, we all coveted the peaches. I should add that it was in Melbourne that a woman informed me, without a glimmer of a smile, "I don't like Poms." I'd guess that the sentiment was true of other Aussies, but I didn't expect to hear it from the wife of a faculty member of the university where Joe had been invited to speak. I've wished since that I'd been quick enough to tell her: "We all need to fight our prejudices."

Melbourne was a handsome city. It had the usual tall buildings downtown, with beautiful metalwork gracing the balconies of the smaller townhouses and apartments. A stroll through the Royal Botanical Garden filled with eucalyptus, gum trees, and other exotics gave me the feeling that I was more "abroad" than I'd ever been.

After Joe had given his lectures, we drove west toward Adelaide where Wilf and Lola Elders were on holiday from California. This was Lola's territory, where she and her brother had grown up on a sheep farm in the Barossa Valley. Lola took us to her natal home, where we met her brother's widow, and her nephew, Tim, who had taken charge of the farm after his father's death. He lived there with his mother, his wife Rose, and their two small girls. As we discovered later, Tim was also a published poet.

The first order of business was a "barbie" with Tim in charge; he cooked lamb chops for us in a grove of magnificent gum trees behind the house, and served them with various homegrown vegetables. After lunch, Lola led us up nearby Pin Hill where from the summit we could see acres of grassland littered with sheep, and beautiful views of the countryside with the Mount Lofty ranges in the distance. Back at the farm I was surprised when Lola showed us a pile of rocks in the middle of the home field and told us that this was where her brother and father were buried.

I believe this is possible in England, too, although I had never come across actual burials outside a cemetery; however, I'm told that the little lane that runs through my brother-in-law's farm in Derbyshire is sprinkled with the ashes of several deceased visitors to the farm's campgrounds.

Lola also took us to visit a friend who lived in the bush. This turned out to be a little like the Canadian bush, but even less green. A few trees surrounded the house, as did a great deal of bare, rocky ground where I looked in vain for my first sight of a kangaroo. The outback, which was even farther away from civilization, was higher, rockier, and with even less vegetation.

Adelaide, pretty and neat, is built on a grid like an American town, and sits on the River Torrens, which, like many of Australia's rivers, appears to flow upside-down: mud on the surface, water underneath. But South Australia was a little too green to match my earlier ideas of the country, although it did have a great many exotic trees with many varieties of gums or eucalypts, some of them huge, misshapen, and up to four hundred years old.

After this visit, it seemed that we had seen a great deal of Australia, but not the Australia I had imagined in England when, as a child, I made deep holes in my father's vegetable garden in an attempt to dig down to the antipodes. Where, I wondered, are the kangaroos and wallabies, the wombats and dingoes?

When we drove west to Melbourne once more and continued north toward the capital Canberra, the "real" Australia began to appear. Our digs at Canberra were outside the city in a dry, red-soiled, bush-like area, where again there were very few trees. As we walked, this turned out, at last, to be a realm of the kangaroo, many of which were hopping languidly about, and cropping the low bushes as if oblivious of us. Some of them had joeys peering out of their pouches; some of these young, looking much too big for such motherly concern. Surely they should have been busy with their own foraging?

Even in this bush-like area it was close enough to the city for us to take a short walk and arrive into its streets very quickly. Canberra, like Washington, DC, was built to accommodate the central government, but unlike Washington it felt to us like a ghost town. We saw only a small part of the city, but although the area we visited had shops and offices, there was hardly any traffic: few cars, no buses, and very few people on the streets. Perhaps everyone was at work, but for whatever reason, the city was so quiet it seemed that its population had been spirited away by aliens. The town covered a wide area, and included, in addition to the city streets, many serene parks and gardens full of blossom.

Our next destination was Perth, in Western Australia, 1,670 miles away. We hadn't enough time to drive there, or the inclination, considering it would have taken us at least four days as the road ran through desert most of the way. Consequently, we flew from Sydney and, from thirty thousand feet, watched the grim landscape pass beneath us. After that, Perth came as a pleasant surprise, with its downtown skyscrapers, handsome government buildings, and wide beaches on the Indian Ocean.

Perth sits on two big rivers: the Murray, and the Swan, home to the famous black swans. We stayed in a small, family-style hotel and explored the town on foot, discovering a park where a line of tall gum trees had been planted to honor the men who died at Gallipoli. It was there we saw the curiously shaped kangaroo paws and the red waratah plants. We also visited the port of Fremantle where the final conference dinner was held in a room overlooking the bay.

The next day we took a ferry to Rottnest, a small island offshore in the Indian Ocean. The island is a reserved area, with one or two small restaurants and B&B-style cottages. Permanent residents are few. One road circles the island, so we hired a couple of bicycles and set off along the coast, admiring views of the Indian Ocean as we pedaled along the limestone bluffs with their pines and tea trees. Out in the bay, bottlenose dolphins dived among turbulent waves. We had been told to look for quokkas on the island, three of which we found hopping among the roadside bush, making odd "quokking" sounds. These marsupials look like little, sharp-faced cats. One of them had a tiny joey in its pouch.

Further along the coast we came across the famous giant osprey nests—giant, not because the birds are particularly large, but because the ospreys return to the same nests each year to add another layer of sticks. Some nests were up to seventy years old.

Rottnest was our last tourist stop in Australia. I had enjoyed the country a great deal; the Australians were friendly (except for those with an aversion to Poms). Nevertheless, the countryside made me feel like an alien in another world. It was so not-England, so not-America, and made me realize how it must have been for those long-ago exiles who were sent far from home for some petty crime, with no hope of return.

After flying back to Sydney, we found that the trek back to England had been made even longer by a war somewhere in Africa, which had turned our route into a no-fly zone. This meant that we touched down first at Singapore, where fierce-looking men carrying enormous guns patrolled the airport. After a three-hour wait, we took off north up the length of Malaysia, crossed over the Himalayas and parts of the Soviet Union to as far north as the Baltic Sea. After that it was west to Norway and south to Heathrow Airport, followed by a train journey to Derbyshire. Our jet lag was formidable, and we spent a couple of weeks recovering before it was time to head west once again.

CHAPTER 40

Travels in Italy

EARLY ONE SUMMER IN the nineties, Joe and I took a trip to Italy, which began in the north with a visit to Romano Rinaldi, one of Joe's graduate students who had become a professor at the University of Modena in the Po Valley near Bologna. There we met his English wife, Jenny, and their two daughters. Romano proudly introduced us not only to his family, his handsome city, and his colleagues, but to its world-famous product: balsamic vinegar. He made us a tasty dressing for our salad that night.

After we said good-bye to the Rinaldis, we drove to Venice with its scattering of islands where we explored the canals, and we walked over the Bridge of Sighs, which reminded us of its namesake that spans the River Cam in Cambridge. We behaved like typical tourists: took a gondola down the Grand Canal; visited the Uffizi, Saint Mark's Square, and the Basilica; and rode a motorboat over the sea to Murano to view the famous glassmaking industry.

After Venice, we drove west to Florence, which, like Rome, is a city of art, red roofs, and ancient history. In the Gallerie dell'Accademia, we admired Michelangelo's David, and afterward took a stroll through town, passing the Duomo and the Ponte Vecchio, and crossing the bridge over the Arno River. Best of all was our visit to the Boboli Gardens high up near the Pitti Palace, where we enjoyed a wide and beautiful view over the red-tiled city.

A later trip to Italy, this time to attend a meeting in Naples, began in Rome where we visited the Vatican and the Sistine Chapel. Having hurried ahead of a mob of sightseers, were able to enjoy the ceiling in peace for three minutes before being surrounded by a chattering crowd. We also strolled about the town enjoying the various fountains, the Coliseum, and the Palatine Hill overlooking the Forum. Rome was a fascinating city, every corner filled with ancient history.

We hired a car in Rome for the two-hour drive south to Naples. I remember the beauty of that early summer morning as we set out: the little hill towns, each with its church on the summit; the countryside below alive with the red bloom of poppies.

We soon discovered that Italian drivers are reckless, with the result that drivers of smaller cars seemed as afraid as I of the mass of metal hurtling down the highway. They cringed along, not in the outside lane, but on the shoulder. Traffic was the same in the city, where running a red light was normal, as was driving on the sidewalk in order to get around slower traffic. Because of a lack of official crossing places, we found that pedestrians had to say a fervent prayer, step out into the roadway, and dodge. After we reached our hotel, we found to our relief that its parking lot was closely guarded day and night, and were assured that it was safe to leave our car there for the duration of our stay.

The conference sessions were held at the Castel Sant'Angelo, a huge, round stone building that sits off the banks of the Tiber.

The Emperor Hadrian built the bridge over the river to the castle in AD 134. (The same Hadrian who constructed the Great North Wall between England and Scotland.) In the early days, it was Hadrian's mausoleum, but eventually it became a fortress used by various popes against a variety of enemies. It was stocked with food, water and wine, as well as arms and the men who wielded them.

Joe and I did a great deal of walking around Naples. Some of the conference organizers warned that this could be as dangerous as driving—they were vague about why this was—but we usually had other delegates with us as we walked, and felt comparatively safe; after all, how bad could this town be, to people used to dealing with the streets of Chicago? However, one day when three of us were walking toward the Castel in order to attend a dinner, Joe on the street side of the sidewalk, another man toward the wall, me in the middle clutching my purse, there was a sudden roar behind us as a motorcyclist mounted the walkway, forced his way between me and the man to my left and grabbed his shoulder bag. There followed a brief tussle in which our friend, a small man, but full of both courage and outrage, gave the motorcyclist a huge shove, which almost brought him off his bike, at which point he thought better of it and roared off, leaving us triumphant but shaken. We felt better when people passing us on the sidewalk raised their shoulders and cupped their hands toward us in gestures of apology.

When the conference ended, Joe and I picked up our car from the guarded lot at the hotel, and made our perilous way out of town, dodging more lawless traffic as we did so; once we even shot through on the red ourselves. We had stopped at a red light as law-abiding citizens are supposed to, when the driver of a large van behind us, crept up to our back bumper and, horn blasting, attempted to push us into the intersection. At the same time, cars to the right and left of us, some on the sidewalk, were running the light, and it shortly became obvious that if we didn't do the same we would be crushed. We ran the light.

Once free of the city, we headed across the bay to Pompeii and Herculaneum, to visit the towns that had been overwhelmed by a volcanic eruption in 79 BC. Several volcanoes reared into the sky along the coast. Pompeii, once a viable community, had been obliterated by volcanic ash; some buildings had been buried under it, and others reduced to little more than their foundations. Some areas have since been dug from the ash, revealing paved roads with footpaths on either side, the remains of public baths and fountains, private houses with frescoes and mosaics still intact, and public buildings, including an amphitheater. We walked for some hours among these ruins and saw the outlines of the bodies of people who had died in the eruption, sprawled about the floors of a house. Their shapes could still be seen where they fell before being buried under the volcanic dust; the forms had later been reinforced with plaster to preserve them. (I have learned recently that the deaths in both Pompeii and Herculaneum are now considered the result, not of smothering by ash or volcanic mud, but of the intense heat.)

After this, we drove down to the coast to visit Herculaneum. Whereas historic Pompeii had been a city of ordinary folk, Herculaneum was the playground of wealthy Romans, their buildings more opulent and less damaged than those of their neighbors living closer to the eruption. Again there were frescoes and other rich decorations including marble statues.

After this, we motored north toward Rome and the airport, trying to ignore other historic sites along the way; had we weakened, we might still be wandering among Italy's myriad historic places.

CHAPTER 41

Arizona

ALTHOUGH IT MIGHT APPEAR otherwise, all this traveling took up only a fraction of our lives. Joe was still busy with teaching and research at the University of Chicago; I with my work for RFB&D. We were making trips to see our girls, Susan in Madison, and Ginnie in New York.

Despite our full lives, Joe and I were able to take a journey to southern Arizona to meet a mineral prospector named Sidney Williams, whom Joe was told might be able to supply him with a mineral he needed for research. The prospector owned a ninety-acre stretch of desert close to the Mexican border, which we approached over fifty miles of dirt road, arriving dustily, late at night, at a jumble of several long, white, one-story buildings. There seemed to be no one about, but suddenly three large dogs surrounded our car, barking and snarling. Because there was a large sign reading "Beware of the Dog," we prudently remained in the car.

After about ten minutes, during which Joe gingerly beeped the horn, a man appeared at the door of one of the buildings. He was about seventy years old, tall, thin, grizzled, his eyes abnormally blue; he turned out to be Williams. He harried the dogs off into a fenced compound, and ushered us inside one of the buildings where he introduced his wife Betty, a small, sturdy-looking woman with gray eyes and abundant gray hair caught up into a twist. She didn't shake my hand, and that's when I noticed that each of her fingers had been reduced to a red stub.

While the men went to the lab next door to discuss minerals, Betty and I sat in a portion of the factory-like building, and attempted to talk. A corner of the room had been set up as their living room, with furniture, the heads of horned animals on the walls, and an African shield with crossed spears over the mantelpiece. (Williams worked in both Africa and South America.)

Betty was extremely shy and talk was difficult, but gradually over the two days we were with them, perhaps because I was careful not to invade her privacy, she began to open up. She told me she worked in the lab as a chemist, although she didn't mention her damaged hands, the fingers of which looked as though they had been badly burned by either chemicals or fire. She also told me that when they set up their company they had named it Globo de Plomo (the Lead Balloon); presumably they'd doubted it would take off. It seemed at least one of them was a joker.

Later in our visit, she took me around all of the labs and explained their work. She also told me of the mile-long racing track they had built out in the desert. One of the cars they drove was a limited-edition Maserati that on one occasion had been used in the making of a film. She also boasted about Sidney's work for the Turkish government, but it was inoffensive, almost child-like boasting.

Because Williams had arrived home that day from Africa and was jet lagged, Joe and I left early to drive via dirt roads and then blacktop, to the small town of Douglas, where the Williams owned a guesthouse. It was one of a group of houses within a few hundred yards of the Mexican border. We knew the number of the building we were looking for, but since no numbers were visible, we decided that because only one house was in darkness it must be the one we sought. Hoping no suspicious homeowner would come out, guns blazing, Joe tried the key Williams had given him, and was relieved to find that it worked.

The house was a small, two-bedroom bungalow, as was common in Chicago; plain and comfortable with all mod cons, and a small front lawn. However, I was a little perturbed to find that there were black, iron grilles over all the windows and on the doors front and back, even though the small, blue-collar town seemed quiet and safe enough. The only building of size was the Gadsden Hotel, which we found later had Tiffany glass windows of desert views and historic scenes of the conquistadores, plus a sweeping staircase leading to the upper floors. It must once have been most elegant.

The next day we went back to the Williamses' home, and while Joe and Sidney again talked science, I kept out of Betty's hair by taking a walk around the property. There I discovered the small racetrack she had told me about, with two fancy cars parked beside it. There was also a small Ramada, a shelter, its walls held up by wooden posts and with a wooden roof. It had comfortable seats from which I could enjoy a fine panorama of the surrounding desert with its cholla and saguaro cacti, and mesquite bushes. The Chiricahua Mountains loomed away in the distance, and I sat there for some time, writing, reading, and occasionally nodding off.

That night we took our hosts to the historic Gadsden Hotel for a thank-you dinner. It was rather run down, but must once have been an elegant meeting place for mine executives, ranchers, and cattlemen. Over dinner, I decided that Williams was the joker in the family who had hoped to gull us two citified innocents. In one of his stories he was out in the desert leading a group of mineralogists, when he heard some of them sharpening their machetes in order to attack him. Joe had heard a similar tale at the conference in Albuquerque, where he was told about a different group whose leader was so unpleasant that the conferees had discussed, jokingly, how to deal with him; a machete attack had not been contemplated. Williams's next story was even less plausible and of doubtful taste; it concerned a local rancher who, he claimed, had killed his girlfriend's children, and then eaten them. Joe and I weren't sure why he told us such a disagreeable tale. Did he think it was funny? Did he actually believe it to be true? Was he merely trying to shock this couple of townies? The rest of the dinner passed a little awkwardly. The food was only marginal, but, since we were paying, I was mollified when the bill came to only $4.85 each.

CHAPTER 42

Bisbee and Beyond

WHEN WE FIRST VISITED the Bisbee copper mines in Arizona back in the early 1970s, it was a scene of total devastation. Mountaintops had been demolished, leaving an area of huge canyon-like depressions, some of them a thousand feet deep, with hundreds of miles of underground workings burrowed into the sides of the eight-hundred-foot cliffs. The bright red walls of the canyons were terraced all the way down to the bottom, and trucks ran along the terraces collecting ore dug from the sides of the mine, and from its tunnels. The noise had been horrific: explosions followed by the scramble of falling rock, roaring bulldozers hauling them around the canyon floors, dozens of truck engines snarling their way down the terraces.

Soon after, the copper ran out, the mines were closed and the area was left desolate: acres of mine waste, heaps of discarded ore, scoured hillsides, and deep pits gouged out of the land. Thousands of men lost their jobs.

In the 1990s, we were astonished to find that the town had become a gentrified tourist mecca. The huge canyons that had been the mines no longer appeared threatening, the mine waste and heaps of discarded ore had been cleared away, and visitors were allowed to stand at the top of the canyons to enjoy the magnificence of the surrounding scenery. In the largest of the depressions, run-off from above had developed into lakes on the floor, and nature had begun to take over: desert plants such as creosote bushes, prickly pear, and ocotillo were again beginning to flourish. Not the Grand Canyon perhaps, but nevertheless a breathtaking scene.

The little town of Bisbee, built higgledy-piggledy on the mile-high hillsides in the manner of a Swiss village, had also recovered. After the loss of jobs in the mine, the area now catered to tourists, and the miners' houses had been refreshed, their bricks sandblasted clean, their woodwork brightened with paint. The old hotel was still standing, all balconies and curlicues in the manner of old western hotels, and the shops and miners' cottages now housed small museums, including one about mining, and the Bisbee Restoration Museum. Little galleries sold Indian jewelry, and in boutiques were cards, perfumes, soaps, jams, and samples of the minerals found embedded in the local copper: turquoise, malachite, azurite and galena among them. There were other unusual developments in the town: it now had a golf course, and if you were that way inclined, it was possible to hire a golf cart in order to take a ghost tour of the area, or indulge in Shamanic healing. A local warned me grimly, "The hippies have moved in"; but the shopkeepers seemed pretty ordinary folk, the little community very attractive.

Joe and I both enjoyed Bisbee. I noted in my journal that the "countryside is ringed by the brown Mule Mountains, the weather a warm seventy to eighty degrees, a welcome respite from the northern Indianan spring that refused to show its face."

From Bisbee, we took the winding, shoulder-less washboard road that rose to eight thousand feet through the Coronado Forest. In the lower parts, live oaks grew on either side of the road, while the higher elevations were home to pinyon pines, sycamores, and redbud. It was cool up there, the crests of the hills snow covered. As we climbed, there were steep drop-offs from the road on either side with vistas to take one's breath away—almost as much as did the road. We passed only two cars before we reached the small town of Coronado and the nearby Chiricahua National Monument, where we left the car and hiked up to Massai Point. It was only a mile walk, but at that height we were soon gasping. There we reached a lookout where the rhyolite pinnacles could be seen at their best: bony white volcanic fingers pointing skyward all around us, the skies a brilliant blue, and on the horizon, clouds trailing curtains of rain. It was a satisfying ending to our latest search for the geology and glorious landscapes of the Southwest.

CHAPTER 43

Madison, Wisconsin

JOE AND I ENJOYED spending time in Madison, Wisconsin, with Sue and family. The winters in Madison weren't much worse (or better) than those in Chicago's Hyde Park, so the extreme cold didn't deter us.

One of the big advantages of visiting Madison in the summer was its proximity to the American Players Theatre, with its outdoor stage in the woods near Spring Green, about an hour's drive west of Madison. The actors were fabulously good, and included Randall Duk Kim who played in Moliere's amusing *Tartuffe*; we also saw Shakespeare's *A Winter's Tale*, which I voted "a long, pedestrian play. Could have been written by anyone." (I can't blame this on youthful folly: I was sixtyish at the time.)

Over the years, we saw many wonderful plays at APT, among them *School for Scandal* and a great many of Shakespeare's plays, including a wonderful *Hamlet* and a production of *King Lear,* again with Kim in the lead. He also played an excellent Shylock in *The Merchant of Venice.*

The theater was out in the country on top of a small hill, where comfortable seats stepped down an incline to the stage. The car park was at the foot of the hill, and a bus ferried people who were unable to walk to the top. We usually took the path that led through a small wood and past a field full of golden rod, sunflowers, and brown-eyed Susans, to the summit. I remember only one occasion on which the play was paused when a rainstorm hit, and we sipped coffee as we waited under cover for it to pass. There is an indoor theater further down the hill used for one-act plays and lectures, but it is not large enough to accommodate the outdoor audiences driven from their seats by the weather.

We heard much music in Madison. Admittedly, the local symphony orchestra was not on the level of the Chicago Symphony—which is rated one of the ten best in the world—but it was acceptable, and over the years became progressively more so. We enjoyed those concerts once a month. Sue was also involved in music, first as a member of the Middleton Choir, and later the University's Choral Union, which on separate occasions sang Brahms, Rutter, Ravel, Vivaldi, and Beethoven, all of them gloriously. There were also several chamber music groups in the town that performed in various churches, some of them very good indeed. And in Sue's Christian Reformed Church every Sunday, talented members of the congregation enhanced the service with the music of piano, violin, viola, guitar, flute, clarinet, and even euphonium. A young male opera student with a beautiful voice often led the hymn singing.

Joe and I spent significant time walking in the parks. At Picnic Point, we took a path that led through a wood down a peninsula that jutted out from the shores of Lake Mendota. We also visited the arboretum, where in spring we enjoyed groves of sweet smelling lilacs, magnolias, and apple blossom. Another ramble included Owen Park, once a farm, now a prairie, which was thick with little bluestem grasses, sunflowers, purple coneflowers, and goldenrod. In autumn, the trees surrounding the park were vivid with color: the red of sumacs, the brilliant yellow of aspens, the red and yellow of maples.

Olbrich Gardens, on the east side of Madison, was particularly fine. Next to the visitor's center was a large glass conservatory containing a tropical rainforest with huge palm trees, orchids, bromeliads, and pitcher plants. Paths wound across the forest floor, and then spiraled up around the walls into the canopy. High above, a waterfall splashed over jagged rocks to join a small stream, full of goldfish, which sparkled on the floor below. The trees were alive with yellow canaries and waxbills, and tiny quail scuttled about in the undergrowth pecking for seeds and insects. Outside were many different gardens: one devoted to roses, others to desert plants, perennials, herbs, grasses, and woodlands. The Thai Pavilion, situated across a bridge over the Yahara River, was donated to Madison by the Thai government. It is a beautiful building decorated with gold leaf, and has curling, eastern-style roofs.

We also enjoyed exploring the university campus, particularly the Memorial Union with its cafeteria and lakeside Terrace where we could sit and enjoy our coffee while we watched the sailboats on Lake Mendota. Nearby was Science Hall where our friend, and Joe's colleague, Bill Bailey, was a professor. Up on Observatory Hill, again overlooking the lake, were two Indian mounds: one representing a bird, the other a turtle. During our first trip out west in 1952, these were the first Indian mounds we came across.

In August 1988 Susan was married to David Werther, who had been Sue's instructor for two courses in theology. The wedding was held at Grace Episcopal Church in downtown Madison. Susan looked lovely in her wedding finery, David handsome in a dark suit and colorful tie, and Ginnie as Maid of Honor in a pretty floral dress. I was escorted to my seat on the arm of David's brother, while Joe waited at the back to escort Sue down the aisle. The wedding was lovely, with music performed by some of Sue's friends: flute, string quartet, and a bass who sang an aria from Bach's St. Matthew Passion. The ceremony was followed by a reception at the Civic Center with a catered dinner and a dance.

While David worked on his PhD in philosophy, Sue continued part-time at the Geology Department, switching from graphics to the Geology Museum, where she worked designing exhibits, giving tours, and running a summer program for kids. She loved working at the museum; her interests in geology, art, teaching, and children had all come together.

On September 9, 1993, a new family member appeared on the scene: Jessica Alice Werther, our first grandchild. When the news came, Joe and I drove north from Chicago to the hospital in Madison, and found Jessica to be, as we had found both our daughters, perfect. She was a sweet, non-fussy baby with her father's fair hair and her mother's serious brown eyes.

At first, Sue kept her hand in at the museum, working a few hours a week and occasionally giving a tour with Jessica in her sling or taking her on field trips with the Geology for Kids pro-gram. But after three years, she let the job go to be a stay-at-home mom, while her husband, David, taught philosophy in the University of Wisconsin-Madison distance education program.

In 1989, after working for seven years for New York book publishers, including Dell and Doubleday, Ginnie began work as an acquiring editor at HarperCollins, where several of her titles were on the *New York Times* bestseller list. She lived on the Upper West Side with her partner, Kathy. In 1994, daughter Katie, was born, and in 1996, John. I cut back my hours at Recording for the Blind and Dyslexic, which allowed Joe and me some lovely long weekends with both of our daughters in Madison and New York City, not to mention the new additions to our family.

In 1997, Ginnie relocated from Manhattan to Boston, where she became a stay-and-home mom to her two, then three, children, while writing and publishing fiction and nonfiction, including a parenting column for the *Boston Globe* Sunday magazine. Kathy made a career switch from the corporate world to become a high school math teacher. Then, in 2002, Meg, our fourth and last grandchild, joined the family.

CHAPTER 44

Travels in France

JOE AND I RETURNED to France in July 2001 (I'm certain of this date only because Joe marked the route on a map and dated it.) We went by way of London, where we visited the usual tourist landmarks: Westminster Bridge and the Houses of Parliament; the Tower; the Millennium Wheel; the ill-fated Dome, ill-fated because the public refused to support it with donations, and when it opened, refused to visit. It is now a very successful tourist attraction. We then took the "Chunnel" to France and headed for Montpelier on the south coast where Joe was to attend an International Zeolite Conference.

Not surprisingly, Montpelier appeared to me to be "very French." It was built of limestone in mid-eighteenth-century style, the buildings five or six stories high with mansard roofs. There was a huge, Classical-style opera house in the main square, and smaller squares that were filled with little sidewalk cafés and people walking leisurely about or sitting at tables, many of them pretending not to watch us interlopers. The people were mostly locals; we seemed to be the only tourists. The vivid blue sky, to the eyes of this northerner, was extraordinary. The only drawback was the large amount of graffiti everywhere; otherwise the streets were beautifully swept and neat. Our hotel and the site of the conference was a large townhouse that was reputed to have belonged to Queen Elena of Italy.

I went on several tours arranged for the conference hangers-on, one to a town named Aigues-Mortes, meaning "dead waters"—that is, salt as opposed to fresh. The walls of the town were perfectly preserved, with guard posts at each corner and a magnificent entry gate. It was built in the thirteenth century for King Louis IX who required a port from which to trade with the Orient, and launch his crusades. The church is also from thirteenth century but with appalling modern stained glass. The inner parts of the town are from the fifteenth through the eighteenth centuries, and had been destroyed many times over, by Burgundians, Huguenots, and other marauders. We learned a grisly tale of a siege by Burgundians, many of whose corpses still lay about the streets after their army had been repulsed. There was nowhere to bury them within the confines of the town, so they were taken to one of the towers, piled inside with a layer of salt between each corpse, and left to rot. The tower is still called the Tower of the Burgundians.

On our way back to Montpellier, we drove through the Camargue country, which is mainly marshland with pools of both salt and fresh water. There we saw many kinds of gulls and ducks, along with flocks of pink flamingoes. It was a birder's heaven. We also saw the famous local bulls, and the magnificent white horses, some of which belonged to local people, others that roamed wild.

We toured a huge cave, or series of caves—les Grottes de Clamouse—that had cathedral-like rooms with stalactites, stalagmites, crystals of various kinds, and much fretted lace-like rock caused by deposits from mineral-rich groundwater. We were underground for an hour, walking a trail cut out of the limestone rock, and gasping at one magnificent view after another. It had not, the Lord be praised, been Disneyfied, but was tastefully lighted and quite silent apart from the sound of dripping water and the shuffle of feet. We then visited Saint Guilhem le Desert deep in a limestone gulley. It seemed to be an artist's retreat, plus a few authentic locals: the old men with their berets, the old women in black. A charming old village with a large church, and narrow streets that twisted down the sides of the gulley.

A less successful trip was when the whole conference visited a farm in the Camargue where the locals staged a bullfight, not the Spanish form but a French version in which young men entered the ring and attempted to get the bulls to attack them. Each jet-black animal had a piece of cloth attached to its huge horns, and the men would snatch the cloth and escape harm by making a tremendous leap over the fence that surrounded the ring. For a while, this was exciting, but then the bulls began to leap the fence into another, surrounding ring. There they ran snorting around it, while the men encouraged them to leap back and attempt to attack them. From then on it seemed possible that a bull could break a leg, and the fight was no longer as innocent as I had believed it to be. The animals began to foam at the mouth and leave quite a lot of hair on the fence as they scrabbled over. The men, however, seemed to be in little danger.

When the conference was over, we joined about thirty delegates and their companions on a field trip to the Auvergne and the Massif Central. A man from Montpellier organized the trip, along with several helpers. Joe and I were among the oldest in the group, and I think it caused a little consternation when we got out of the bus and prepared to hike up to a quarry and then to the crest of a nearby volcano. One older woman elected to stay on the bus, but, dammit, we had come on a field trip! Not that anything was said, but as I followed the group up the hill, I realized that one of the helpers had been assigned as a sort of herdsman to make sure that no one, particularly not this ancient woman, collapsed on the way. I like to take my time on geological expeditions in order to look at the scenery, the flowers, the trees, as well as the rock formations. Geologists can spend hours chipping at bits of rock, and I usually have plenty of time to catch up with the main body. Today, however, this wasn't to be; I was chivvied along and arrived at the site more or less with the others before I could do my customary gazing about.

The countryside just north of Montpellier consists of limestone hills with sharp peaks and deep gullies, unlike the more rounded Derbyshire hills. The vegetation was also quite sparse and consisted of rosemary and other low-lying herbs. Further north, we came to the peak of our journey where we spent an evening on the top of the Puy de Dôme, one of the highest volcanoes in France. There, after a splendid dinner at the restaurant at the top, we circumnavigated the summit in order to take in the breathtaking views. Hang gliding was pioneered there and the air above us held a flock of bodies spiraling on the updrafts. (I wished I were younger, braver, and could have a go.) Far below we saw the tops of lesser volcanoes clothed in brilliant green grass, with various sized hollows that were their long-dead craters. We stayed that night at a nearby town named Chaude Aigue (warm water), where the steep little town is given over to hot springs, and in which there were many old folk taking the waters. It was an old town in more ways than one. We were told that all the little towns in the area are losing their young folk because there are few jobs and not enough excitement; we saw very few young people on the streets, which may be why the townsfolk were friendly and eagerly invited us to return.

We had been promised a surprise after dinner and I guessed it would turn out to be dancing girls. And so it was, in a way. As we were finishing our glasses of wine, a group of dancers entered the room, many of whom would never see sixty-five again. The men were dressed in dark suits, Spanish-style hats and neckerchiefs, the women in long black dresses with bunches of flowers at the bosom. The band consisted of six men flourishing five accordions and one French-style bagpipe. It had no chanter: the reed through which, in Scotland, the tune is played alongside the sound of the drones.

The old folks danced up a storm, doing local country-dances. There must have been something in the local water because they kept on and on to much applause. After a while we were invited to join in, which we did—very badly. After Joe kissed the old lady who was his partner on both cheeks, they elected him a member of the group, gave him a Spanish hat and a scarf, and included him in the final dance. (As we say in Derbyshire, Joe "was a devil when he'd had chips"; even more so when he'd had a glass or two of wine.) It was a warm, convivial evening. The next morning, I felt a little sad when we were accosted by some of the townspeople as we headed for our bus. "You're leaving? Already?" They were rooting for their little town.

CHAPTER 45

The Long Good-bye

IN THE SUMMER OF 2001, it was our fiftieth wedding anniversary, and Ginnie arranged a party in our Derbyshire village to celebrate. She booked a large room at The Jovial Dutchman, the Crich pub that had been named in honor of the men from Holland who built the Cromford canal in the early 1790s to service Richard Arkwright's mill and other businesses in the valley. It was a joyful evening. Ginnie had invited many friends and relatives from both sides of the family, and brought children Katie, aged seven, and John, aged five with her. Sue, David, and Jessica, aged eight, flew over for the occasion. We enjoyed good food, and much beer was consumed at the bar.

A little after this, what Dickens called "the winter of life" began to trouble our family. At first the weather was merely autumnal. I had noticed that Joe's driving had become less precise, and when he brought the car to a halt in our driveway, he seemed to take much longer than usual to undo his seatbelt, open the door of the car, and step out. At first this pause was very slight, and I wondered for some time if I were imagining things. But after a while, the pause became more prolonged and it was obvious that Joe's walking was now more hesitant.

Joe was still able to drive short distances, and we continued make the three-hour trip to visit Susan in Madison and the eighteen-hour drive to Ginnie on the East Coast by taking turns behind the wheel and driving the route we had taken several times before: a glorious road that runs through northern Ohio, Pennsylvania, and New York, over the Appalachians and into New England.

In 2003, he was diagnosed with bladder cancer—a mild case, the doctor assured us, as though this were possible. Subsequently, he had an operation and was told he had some small growths, which "will have to be watched." We would have to wait for three months and test them again. Meanwhile, Joe's speech was becoming slurred, his walking more erratic, and one arm often seemed somewhat paralyzed. He still insisted on driving, and I was on tenterhooks until I persuaded him to let me drive most of the time.

In 2004, Joe was diagnosed with Parkinson's disease. He handled the news in the way he handled all of life's setbacks: with courage, common sense, and determination. There was no need for despair, he assured me; doctors were working even then to find a cure. Besides, the malady affected people in different ways; he could be one of the lucky ones whose symptoms remain minor. We must read what the medical researchers had to say about it; we must look at the evidence. He was prescribed L-dopa, and for a while seemed to be better for it. He bought books and began to study his illness, as he'd studied his science. Above all, he went on with both his life and his research. A few years before, he had organized a conference in San Francisco on the danger to human life of asteroids, earthquakes, and volcanoes. At the time of his illness, he was also concerned with the threat to human life of man-made climate change, and began to write a book about that and other threats to the world. At the same time, he continued his work at the Lab.

After Joe's diagnosis, I retired from RFB&D, but kept involved, volunteering at the downtown Chicago studio a couple of times a week. Life went on as if normal. However, after another year, it became impossible for any of us, even Joe, to deny that his illness was getting worse, and in 2005 he brought up the idea that we should sell our Beverly Shores home and go to live near our daughters, six months in Massachusetts with Ginnie, where she and her family had moved in 1997, and six in Wisconsin. We knew we would be happy close to either of the girls, and we enjoyed both Boston and Madison. Ginnie and Sue seemed happy we were contemplating such an arrangement, but Ginnie now had three children, with the birth of Meg in 2002, and space in her house was limited; we would need her to find an apartment for us in Brookline.

Sue, with one child, would have enough room for us in her house since there was a spare bedroom with a bathroom next to it; however, the tiny dining area at the end of the kitchen was too small to accommodate all five of us at the same meal. Consequently, as well as buying an apartment in Brookline two doors away from Ginnie's condo, we gave Sue and David money so that they could have a dining room built next to their kitchen, add a room and an extra bathroom in the basement, and build a deck onto the house.

In 2005, we put Ballantrae House, our home for almost thirty years, in the hands of a local real-estate broker, and after a short while she sent us potential buyers: two men who loved the house and its location overlooking Lake Michigan. There was only one thing they didn't love: the tan-colored, viscous, stretchy material that Joe had squirted between every single vertical board that comprised the outside of the house.

There was no reason for Joe to have "sealed" these boards; they were water- and air-tight. But Joe with a tool was a man on a mission. With a pair of clippers in hand he couldn't help himself from cutting back roses to within an inch of their life, as his niece Julie discovered when she asked him to trim her roses. With a hammer in his hands, no nail was safe from him. And with a caulk gun, Joe went to town, filling every possible crack, even those where there was no possible reason for doing so.

Be that as it may, Joe had done his usual comprehensive job on the outside of our house, so that there were long stretches of gross, mucus-looking material between every single board on the house. The prospective buyers took a close look at the house, couldn't imagine anyone putting this ugly material all over if there were no reason for it, and promptly canceled their offer. In order that this not happen again, Ginnie, who arrived the next week, spent most of two days pulling the snot-like material off the house for the next possible buyer, carefully calibrating which room Joe was in, and moving to the opposite side of the house so he wouldn't see her undoing all of his work.

Finally, a woman who seemed not at all deterred by what I thought was the huge sum we had been advised to ask for the house made an offer. And so, Ballantrae House was sold.

I did the packing by first collecting a great many used cardboard boxes in which to send dishes, bed linens, and personal belongings to the apartment Ginnie had found for us in Brookline. I also decided which furniture would fit in our new quarters, what we would need in Madison, what Virginia could use, and which pieces to sell.

The apartment in Brookline was across a small triangular park near Ginnie's house, and was on the first floor of a three-unit condominium, a "Boston triple-decker." It was built Massachusetts-style, its siding painted blue, each floor having a small deck that overlooked the park. It had two bedrooms, a bathroom, a kitchen with space for a small breakfast table, a dining room, and a living room. I sent some of the furniture to Madison for use in the new dining room; the items I kept fit the Brookline space well. In the basement, there was room for our overflow of shelves and boxes near the communal washer and dryer. We had Joe's colleague drive our car to Madison, where Susan sold it, and Joe and I took a flight to our new life in Brookline.

Despite missing Hyde Park and Beverly Shores, our new digs suited us very well, especially after I discovered that in Brookline we could take walks through nearby parks. Also, it was good to be near Ginnie and her family, although, since the two oldest, Katie and John, were teenagers, a trifle noisy. After a particularly loud outburst, I shocked them all by telling the children, English style, to "shut up!" It turned out that to use that phrase was "unacceptable behavior" in America. I hope everyone has recovered.

Once settled in Brookline, Joe continued to work on his book titled *Living Safely*, and I continued with my mystery, *Death in the Dunes*, and my first memoir, *A Pennine Childhood*. I joined Ginnie in her various activities, going to church with her and Meg who was too young for her rebellion against religion to carry much weight. The older two claimed to be atheists and refused to come with us, except, under pressure, at Christmas and Easter.

We enjoyed walks along the footpath beside the Muddy River, which stretches for miles, and another around Jamaica Pond, a small lake surrounded by woods with an island where cormorants gather along with wild geese, gulls, and many different kinds of duck. We often counted up to six turtles sunning themselves on a log that extends out into the pond. During our many previous trips to visit Ginnie and her family in Brookline, Joe and I often drove there for a stroll. Ginnie had a community garden in a large park not too far from the pond, and on our visits, Joe often helped with the digging, planting, weeding, and watering.

I also met Ginnie's friends, and with her joined a mystery book group that met at the local library within walking distance of our apartment, and became a member of a memoir-writing group at the local Senior Center. Apart from Joe's illness, life was good.

CHAPTER 46

Darkness Falls

EVENTUALLY, JOE'S ILLNESS BECAME worse. He had to give up driving, and his walking deteriorated until he needed to use a walker when we went out to the library or to a local restaurant. Later, he began having trouble swallowing his food, even the hot soups and other soft foods I made him.

In late February 2005, just ten weeks after we moved to Brookline, Massachusetts, Joe fell and broke his hip. At the hospital, he underwent a stress test to see if his heart was strong enough for him to undergo hip surgery. When the test was administered, he had a heart attack, and was immediately taken to the operating room where he had quintuple bypass surgery. Not long after, they operated on his hip. Despite having undergone two major surgeries in quick succession, they soon had him up and walking, and doing physical therapy to help him regain his strength.

During the next fourteen months, Joe had four more heart attacks, and fell several times. One time, in the middle of the night, he staggered from his bedroom with blood streaming from a cut on his forehead, having fallen against a metal handrail attached to the wall. Each time I called an ambulance, which in Brookline meant that the fire department turned up; the men claimed they had more training than the ambulance personnel! Every trip to the hospital was followed by several weeks or a month at a rehabilitation center close to downtown Boston and the Charles River, where Ginnie and I visited nearly every day, sometimes taking Joe for a ride in his wheelchair along the riverside path.

Joe, still stoic in the face of all these terrible setbacks, returned home from each of his times at the hospital and rehab, where it became obvious that I would now need more help in caring for him. I hired a woman to come in during the morning to help him shower and dress, and, with Ginnie's help, looked after him from 10:00 a.m. until 10:00 p.m., when a second woman arrived to help him to bed and to cover the night hours. Later, he had assistance from a physical therapist who helped him with his walking, and a speech therapist when talking had become too difficult. During all this, Joe's courage was phenomenal and he continued to work on his book, which certainly helped me to cope when I began to feel overwhelmed by despair. Virginia has since written of her father, "I have never witnessed such stoicism in the face of so much suffering." Amen to that.

Joe was admitted to hospital for what proved to be the last time in the spring of 2007. Sue had come to be with us during that last, heartbreaking week. One day, Joe seemed so low that we decided Ginnie and I would stay overnight at the hospital, while Sue returned to the apartment. Joe had been sharing a room with another man, but that night Ginnie managed to arrange for Joe's companion to be moved to another room, pulled the other bed next to Joe's so I could lie next to him, and begged a cot for herself. Joe had been fed liquids through a tube in his nose, but he pulled it out several times. That was when an end-of-life counselor told us it would be best to remove the feeding tube for good and stop giving him fluids. I must have been in denial because, even then, I didn't realize, as I lay beside Joe, holding his hand, how close he was to the end. Nevertheless, early on the morning of Good Friday, April 7, 2007, very quietly, Joe left us. After he died, Ginnie showed me a view out the hospital window of a full moon, with steam from a hospital chimney rippling over its surface up into the blackness of the night. It was as though Joe's indomitable spirit were rising with it.

That summer we took my lad home to Derbyshire. Our daughters and their families, Ginnie, Kathy, Katie, John, and Meg, born in 2002, and Susan, David, and Jessica came over from America. Many relatives of Joe's, including his brother and sister and their families, along with his numerous cousins, nieces and nephews, and a few of mine, came to the funeral at St. Mary's church in Crich, the village where Joe was born. There were also colleagues in attendance, including friends Barry Dawson from Edinburgh University, who gave the eulogy (Barry died in January 2013), Ian Parsons, also from Edinburgh, Henry Emeleus from Durham, and Mike Bown from Cambridge and his daughter Sally Bown Herbert from London. Joe's sister Hilary arranged a reception afterward at the Tramway Museum in the old quarry at Crich. Joe's colleague, Peter Wyllie, from both Penn State and the University of Chicago, wrote a lovely tribute to Joe for the National Academy of Sciences, which can be found at http://www.nasonline.org/publications/biographical-memoirs/memoir-pdfs/smith-joseph-v.pdf.

Later, in October 2007, the Department of Geophysical Sciences at the University of Chicago held a symposium in Joe's honor that was attended by his colleagues and former students from all over the world. To his many colleagues, his students from his over fifty years of teaching, and his family, Joe was deeply missed.

CHAPTER 47

Bagbie Cottage

SHORTLY AFTER JOE'S FUNERAL, my sister Beryl and her husband Rick invited me to go with them for a week to Bagbie, their cottage overlooking the sea in Galloway, southwest Scotland. This area had been my Mecca ever since childhood. I had spent many a summer holiday with my parents, visiting Uncle Gib and Auntie Rose in their cottage at Polbae on the estate of a Major Fox, ten miles north of Newton Stewart. Uncle Gib had been a sergeant in the Major's regiment during the First World War, and took the position of gamekeeper after peace came.

He and my father were good friends. Dad loved to fish, and Uncle Gib would take him over the moors to various lochs; on other occasions they would go to town. One day, Uncle Gib harnessed the old horse to its cart, and the two set out by way of the moor, and headed for Newton Stewart. Dad planned to visit his cousin in the town, and stop in at the post office for stamps as he had to send a report to his company, General Refractories. Why didn't Dad drive his car? I wondered. It was wartime, so perhaps he was short of petrol. But Aunt Rose knew what they were up to. "Don't spend *all* your time at the King's Head," she warned. They must have spent most of their time in that hostelry, because by the time they hit the moorland road that afternoon, the horse was in charge of their route. It was quite some time before Dad stopped snoring and raised his head to find they were surrounded by completely different scenery from that which had graced their journey that morning. It took a while to rouse Uncle Gib, turn the horse and cart around and start heading in the right direction. When they finally arrived at Polbae, Aunt Rose took one look at the revelers, seized the two bottles of Glenfiddich Uncle Gib had stashed under the front seat, and, with a wink at me, hurried off with them to her pantry, where she buried them deep in the barrel of flour she kept for her baking.

In my youth, I had wandered the moors and nearby lochs in a daze of delight, glorying in the scent of bog myrtle and heather, the low, green hills in the distance, the shimmer of silver birch trees along the shore of the little Bladnoch River. I embraced those trees as though they were friends. There were also the birds: ducks and occasional cormorants on the little lochs; curlews, and huge buzzards with their raucous cries, over the moor; and the occasional pheasant among the ferns surrounding the lochs. I would sometimes spend all day in wandering among these delights, so that a local shepherd would report to my parents that he'd seen the "lassie over toward Maberry," a loch some distance from Polbae.

There was also a "wee burn," (a small stream) that ran past the Major's large house and Polbae cottage, and the footbridge that spanned the stream where I carved a shamrock and the initials PF. This was my memorial for Paddy Finucane, an Irishman, who had flown his RAF Spitfire on Britain's behalf in the Second

World War, until he was shot down over the English Channel. "Bren, you didn't even know the lad," my mother protested when I wept.

As a child, I would wander farther along the little road, passing the gardener's cottage on the way—Uncle Gib called the gardener "Pig Lugs" (Pig Ears); obviously he didn't care for him. I was headed for The Derry, where Peter Dewar lived with his wife Netty, the Byerses' eldest daughter, and his children. Mrs. Byers, Netty's mother, was a tough old bird who ruled her family with an iron fist. When her adult children were noisy at table, she would order, "Be quiet! Your father's speakin'."

I had a calming week at Bagbie with Beryl and Rick. The weather was mainly fine with outbreaks of showers: typically Scottish. One day, we drove out to Polbae, where Rick persuaded the people living there to invite us inside. It was strange, and sad, to see Uncle Gib and Aunt Rose's home again where I had spent so many happy summer days. At Bagbie, we also took strolls down the hill to Castle farm, which had been built next to an ancient fort, and up the hill to another farm, Daffin, owned by a French couple. We also drove to Galloway House, near Garlieston, and walked through the nearby woods to the coast where we stopped for lunch. From there, we drove to Wigton, which, it turned out, was Scotland's National Book Town. It has at least eleven bookstores, some with cafés, and one book warehouse. On the way home, we picked up salmon from a friend, who was in charge of the nets that spanned River Cree where it met the Atlantic.

The next day, we drove to the Stewartry Museum, which had what I decided was a "moderate art show," but also to see a new exhibit of Galloway's involvement with the slave trade—of which I'd been ignorant. Glasgow, and other Wigtonshire towns along the River Clyde, had been involved in slavery since the sixteenth century, when copper, guns, and rum were shipped to eastern Africa. These goods were used to buy slaves, who were taken to the east coast of America, where they were sold to companies producing sugar, tobacco, rum, and cotton, all of which were afterward taken back to Britain. This was called The Triangular Trade.

That evening, we had an excellent dinner at the Masonic Hotel in Gatehouse, and early next morning left for home, after what had been for me a restorative visit. Rick and Beryl were leaving at the end of the week for New Zealand, which made me doubly grateful to them.

CHAPTER 48

Iceland

With Lola Elders at an Icelandic "mud pot."

FOR AT LEAST A year after Joe's death, I was numb, but kept on with my usual routines: reading for RFB&D in Cambridge, looking after our garden, taking walks with Ginnie; nevertheless, nothing seemed real. However, gradually, over the years, life began to come back. It wasn't the same, of course, and never would be, but it would have to do. What helped was that I was living close to either Ginnie and family in Brookline, or with Sue and hers in Madison, which is what Joe and I had planned when we left Chicago. We never voiced what we both privately knew: how life would be for the survivor when one of us was no longer around. Joe had been a great companion: loving, quirky, remote when buried in his work, supportive all the time. Becoming used to being without him was not easy.

I continued to go home to England every summer with Ginnie and family, staying in Holly Cottage at Crich Town End, the old surgery in Crich that had become a B&B, and other places nearby. There we visited family and old friends, and once Susan and family came over, along with a couple from Belgium.

Once I flew out to Riverside, California, to stay with Lola and Wilf Elders—my Aussie friend and her English husband whom we met in Chicago. Their house is in the country, a dry area with low bushes and desert plants amid a circle of bare craggy hills. One morning we climbed a grassy footpath to the summit of the nearest hill from where we could look down over a vista of orange groves.

In 2009, Lola invited me to go with her to Iceland, and this wonderful trip helped bring me back to life some more.

Lola's husband, Wilf, had worked on Iceland's Deep Drilling Project for some years, helping the Icelandic government by seeking supercritical temperatures in the steam found below Iceland's volcanic crust. He was due to visit and give the project the benefit of his expertise, and Lola was to go along for the ride.

Lola and I flew together from Boston to the airport of Keflavik, south of Reykjavik, Iceland's capital, where Omar, Wilf's colleague, picked us up at the airport. As we drove toward the capital, the countryside was a revelation; in fact, it seemed there *was* no countryside, only volcanic rocks in all directions, some heaped beside the road in a tumble of boulders, some forming low, craggy hills, a few of them coated in green moss. I thought how Joe would have loved those rocks. I came across greener areas later, but that first impression of Iceland as a rocky wilderness, turned out to be true of about two-thirds of that northern land.

Our first stop in Reykjavik was at a guesthouse full of young people, where we stayed overnight to get over our jet lag. The next morning, we enjoyed an Icelandic breakfast of oatmeal, thick yogurt, and the choice of meat dishes, while surrounded by students talking in languages from around the world. Afterward, with Lola as guide, the two of us set out to explore the town. I found Reykjavik to be a low-key, comfortable place, a more northerly Matlock, the town in Derbyshire where I attended secondary school. The town's only tall building, the large white cathedral, Halgrimskirkja, stands on the tallest hill in the city. We climbed the spire in order to get the best, if not the only, panoramic view of the town with its brightly painted houses and their tiny gardens. The apartment houses were no more than four stories tall, often with paintings on their longer, off-street sides, which depicted butterflies or nesting birds, and once a snake that appeared to slide from a hole in the wall of the house. Many of the structures were wooden and had corrugated iron roofs; others had corrugated iron walls as well. All the houses were painted, some in bright blues or greens, others in a darker red. I found them most attractive, despite my dislike of corrugated iron, which in Britain is used mostly in industrial areas and by farmers for the occasional barn. Lola wasn't troubled by this because corrugated iron is widely used in Australian houses, possibly for the reason it is used in Iceland: the scarcity of trees. According to historians, Iceland was once a well-wooded land until, around AD 870, the first Viking settlers arrived, and over the years built their ships and houses of wood, and used wood as fuel for their log fires. It was not long before Iceland became virtually treeless and the Vikings had to import their building material and fuel from Norway.

One day, Lola and I took an amble along a seaside walk in order to view the Solar Boat, a shining metal replica of a Viking ship that stands on a plinth beside the sea, a symbol of Iceland's early maritime history. There are many ports in and around Reykjavik, where large oceangoing ships are berthed, and that morning navy ships from many different countries were docked, the streets swarming with sailors. One man told us that it was the annual Sailor's Day, when the visiting crews played soccer against each other. The streets were alive with sailors on shore leave, and ships from many European nations crowded the ports and sea-lanes, buried in flags and hooting like angry elephants. We noticed many orange-clad men and women clogging the streets, and were told that they had come to support the Dutch navy.

The next evening, Sigrun, Omar's wife, invited us for dinner. Their daughter joined us and it turned out that both women had been flight attendants for Iceland Air. Sigrun and Omar were excellent hosts, and Sigrun produced a tasty dinner. She took us to the Botanic Garden the next day where we had lunch and enjoyed the garden's Icelandic flowers and shrubs. There were many little shops in town, and in the afternoon, in a place called Sunna, we walked along the waterfront where we saw the famous whooping swans. Turning away from the ocean view, we came across a cemetery with many rowan trees, dandelions, and a few purple primroses. Some of the graves were dolmans, or portal tombs, that had tall lava pillars as markers above them. Nearby, at the City Museum, we saw the remains of one of the town's oldest houses, still sitting in its original position. Built in 871, it had sod walls and a fire pit in its center.

The next day, Lola and I loaded up the car and headed east on Route 1 for the beginning of our counterclockwise tour around the island. The road runs close to the coast for much of the way, and is bordered on its southern, landward side by volcanoes and their high lava cliffs. In one area I counted evidence of at least nine different eruptions on one mountain face. We saw herds of wild deer feeding on the short grasses under the cliffs. To seaward were more grasslands, where we saw cattle, flocks of sheep, both white and black, and fields full of grazing Icelandic horses. (They look like Shetland ponies, but some Icelanders become huffy if you call them that.) The small farms often had sod roofs, and we passed one ancient church from the seventeen hundreds that had sod for both walls and roof, and was built so low it appeared to be crouching into the earth. The inside of the church was tiny, with benches on either side of a simple wooden altar.

As we drove, we ran into torrential rain and a gale force wind that slewed us sideways. Huge boulders that had slumped down from the cliffs above had been moved to the edge of the road, forming a barrier to prevent subsequent falls from hitting passing cars.

After a while, the rain stopped and the sun came out, making the little fjords on the coast look as blue as the Mediterranean. Again, we saw red-roofed farms along the shore, snow-covered volcanoes inland, and many little rivers and waterfalls flowing down the face of the cliffs, some mesa-shaped, others conical with black lava scree, others stepped like Indian temples.

At one place under the cliffs, we again saw reindeer, and three enormous, goat-like creatures with huge horns; no one could tell us what they were. I recently discovered that they are called "Icelandic goats" (*Capra aegagrus hircus*), and date back eleven hundred years in Iceland. The island has no indigenous animals: no rabbits, squirrels, or native deer. There is the Arctic fox, and little else; the animals we saw had all been introduced.

There is a lot of local plant life, although we were told that a good half of it consists of mosses. Among the many different grasses, we spotted campion and some heather in hillier places. Along the roadside lower down were introduced species, such as dandelions, buttercups, marsh marigolds, blue Icelandic poppies, and masses of lupines that were taking over the roadsides. There were very few indigenous trees left; most of the survivors were birch or aspen, stunted and twisted. A forestry scheme is underway in several places in which birches, pines, and aspens are being planted.

The hundreds of waterfalls that cascade over the cliffs on the landward side of the coast road formed when volcanoes erupted under a huge glacier that covers the surrounding hills. Iceland has three glaciers, the largest one near the south coast, Vatnajöckull, and two smaller ones toward the northwest. Further along the road we saw more dramatic evidence of glacial melting when we came across a huge outwash plain and the twisted remains of a road and a mile-long metal bridge. In 1996, a volcano again erupted beneath Vatnajöckull, causing its ice to melt and water to cascade down over the flood plain in such a torrent that it ripped out both the bridge and the road for a considerable distance. These had since been rebuilt, with a parking lot alongside the glacial river, where we got out to have a closer look. The glacier melts frequently, enough to form the torrents that constantly run down to the sea. Where the bridge was destroyed is the site of one of the largest flows. It runs through a wide, graveled floodplain crammed with icebergs broken off the front of the glacier. The water was a dull gray, the icebergs sometimes blue, sometimes almost translucent, one or two jet-black with lava dust. We walked up the valley to where the runoff had eroded a cleft through the lava cliff, to form the river that surged toward the sea. As we traveled farther east, beyond the influence of the glacier, we began to see more green, because in addition to grassy areas, the lava boulders were covered with a brilliant moss.

At the southeast corner of the island where there are many fjords, we turned inland and north to Egilsstaðir. Now, the terrain changed drastically, the valleys widening where glaciation had scoured them out, the sides of the mountains gentler with no tumbled boulders littering the valley floor. We were still in volcanic terrain, but it was very different: higher up, and again with very little vegetation. There were also small canyons where river water from the glacier had eroded the lava. Losing height, we spotted a series of small cairns at fifty-foot intervals along a valley, rather like those in Scotland, which presumably helped people find their way before there were roads. Toward Lake Mývatn, steam fields appeared, which gave the air the smell of sulfur and turned nearby fields pink and green.

We took rooms at the hotel near the lake before we walked out to look at the local church. In 1790, it had been almost surrounded by lava during an eruption; fortunately, the flow separated into two arms, one to the left and one to the right of the building, leaving it unscathed. Afterward we walked on a footpath made through the lava field next to the lake, where we saw loons and mergansers in the unbelievably clear water, and beyond them snow-covered hills with clouds and sunshine in the background.

On the last day of May, we drove to a small nature reserve at Hofdi, a peninsula on the east side of Lake Mývatn, where the silver birches were only just coming into leaf, and there were two well-kept gardens. The lake had areas where castle-like structures made of lava, stretched across portions of its surface. At the other end of the lake we came across little pseudocalderas, small hummocks where steam had vented, causing their tops to slump into tiny craters like miniature volcanoes.

We left Mývatn on June 3. Our next stop was at Iceland's largest waterfall, Godafoss, the place where a "lawspeaker" named Ljosvetningagoi in the year 1000, believing that Iceland should be Christian, threw statues of the old Norse gods into the Skalfandafljot River, which runs into the sea. Even from the parking lot, the noise of the waterfall was deafening, and after we had walked close enough to see it we understood why. The Godafoss consists of two waterfalls side by side where two cliffs meet at a ninety-degree angle. The amount of water is prodigious, and that, plus its height of twelve meters and its width of thirty, explained that huge roar. A rainbow, caused by light passing through spray from the waterfall, added to the glory of the scene. We also visited the Gulfoss with its huge waterfall. There were geysers and mud pots nearby, similar to those Joe and I saw in Yellowstone, although the underlying hotspot, instead of being "only" forty miles across as in America, underlies the whole country of Iceland. Of course we had to experience bathing in one of Iceland's many hot-water pools: a blissfully relaxing experience. Along the north coast, at the town of Laufás, we again came across buildings made entirely of sod, in this case a row of tenth-century houses that were being renovated; probably as a tourist attraction.

Further along the coast, we visited Thingvellir, a small town that had been the site of the first Icelandic Parliament from AD 930 to the end of the eighteenth century. The remains of the buildings sat in a wide plain, which spreads down to the sea with hills on the landward side. There were geysers nearby, both at Geysir and Thingvellir. Geysir gave its name to geysers all over the world.

For me, most interesting was the fact that we were standing on the Mid-Atlantic Ridge that runs north-east to south-west through the country, continuing southwest along the floor of the

Atlantic Ocean for thousands of miles. This is where the North American plate, moving west, parts company with the Eurasian plate, moving east. In Iceland, the ridge runs through a narrow defile with high lava cliffs on either side, and is the actual site of the earliest parliamentary meetings.

That day, we visited the deep drilling area where Wilf was employed, and after having lunch in the canteen, we kitted up in bright yellow vests and hard hats in order to have a closer look at the rig. This consisted of a high, steel structure rather like a gigantic ladder above the drill, which was already a considerable way down into the earth. It had not yet hit either water or steam. We then visited Viti, a crater with deep blue water and precipitous sides, and afterward another steam field where jets of steam were forming small pyramids of pink and yellow minerals, the bad smells catching our throats. There were other areas where hot, black mud roiled, shooting skyward before falling back into dark pools.

Here, the weather warmed somewhat, although the wind was still bitter. Wilf came and drove us to the rig to collect Laura, his student, then back to Route l and the turnoff to Dettifoss, a waterfall in a deep canyon. Basalt formed the top of the falls, and also the canyon beside the turbulent river; its mists helped produced two perfect rainbows, and we took a strenuous walk down steps to the bottom of the valley so that Lola could take photographs.

After this, we left our hotel at Reykjalid and drove again to Mývatn and over the mountains. The countryside here had wider valleys with snow-covered volcanoes in the distance. The grasslands were dotted with sheep, and nearby were enormous round enclosures divided by inner fences into small triangular areas within the circle. Different shepherds owned, or perhaps rented, the enclosures where they brought their animals to be auctioned.

On our way south toward Reykjavik and the airport, we stayed with Lola's friend Hrefna Kristmannsdottir, who had invited us to stay with her at her charming, Swedish-style house. Hrefna was very welcoming, and the first evening she introduced us to her outdoor hot tub, which was relaxing—as long as we kept only our heads above the water to stop the outside air from freezing our bones. The next day, she took us to the lava tunnels at Hallmundarhraun, a chilly experience due to an icy wind blowing off the nearby glacier. There was much moss in the area, a few small wild flowers, the only trees pussy willows no bigger than ground cover.

The waterfall she took us to, the Hraunfossar, was different from others we had visited in that its icy blue waters, trapped underground beneath layers of volcanic rock, did not emerge over the lip of the cliff, but seeped from between layers of rock several yards beneath the surface. There was much more green here, mainly grasses, silver birch trees, and birches with brown bark; these were fully grown but barely ten feet tall.

After returning our rental car, we took a bus trip to Nesjavellir Hraunfossar (*vellir* means valley) where a geothermal operation produces electricity from the steam within the earth, and supplies hot water to neighboring houses.

On our last day in Iceland, we again wandered about Reykjavik, enjoying its harbor views and taking more photographs. At lunch, we met Swanhilde, Hferna's adopted Vietnamese daughter, a likeable, humorous, no-nonsense woman. We later met Sigrun who took us to a public park filled with hefty, Picasso-like statues and lovely gardens. A quietly happy ending to what had been, for me, an exciting and memorable introduction to Iceland. Thank you, Lola.

CHAPTER 49

Eastward Ho! Home to England

ON A WEDNESDAY NIGHT in early September 2011, while I was staying in Madison with Susan's family, I received a telephone call from Ginnie with exciting news. Her older daughter Katie, then sixteen, had been accepted to England's top Sixth-Form College (equivalent to the American junior and senior years of high school). The best part: it was located in Cambridge, where Joe had gone to University and then worked at the Cavendish Laboratory, and where we lived when the girls were young and to which we almost moved in 1977.

Ginnie, Katie, and her younger daughter, Meg, seven, were moving to Cambridge for one or two years. Her son John had already started at a prep school in the White Mountains of New Hampshire, and Kathy would visit him regularly. Ginnie and the girls would be flying to London on Saturday, three mornings hence, and school would begin for Katie on Monday.

Ginnie, the girls, and I had spent the summer in Derbyshire, doing our usual summer things: Ginnie helping with the hay-making on the farm, the girls spending time with their cousins, and all of us going for walks, to the great estate of Chatsworth, spending time with our relations, and visiting Mike Bown and his daughters in Cambridge. When we returned to Boston in August, I had a one-week holiday with Ginnie's entire family at the condo we rented in Provincetown, on the tip of Cape Cod, and then I flew to Wisconsin to spend several months with Susan and family.

While we were in England that summer, Ginnie had read about Hills Road Sixth Form College in the *Guardian* newspaper and mentioned it to Katie. Katie, always up for an adventure, thought she'd give it a shot. In early August, she sent in an application. Ginnie decided not to inform me that Katie was applying to a school in England, because it was highly unlikely that she would be accepted, especially since she wasn't a Cambridge resident or UK citizen, or even living in England. Beyond that, it was now August and the applications had been due last March.

But the admissions director at Hills Road must have seen something in Katie, because on that Wednesday before school began the next Monday, Katie learned she was accepted. She had already begun her junior year of high school, and Meg had begun third grade. But still, an adventure awaited, so Ginnie quickly packed up the family with one suitcase each, and on Saturday morning, they hurled themselves on a plane to Heathrow.

Our old friend, Mike Bown, who had worked with Joe at the Cavendish Laboratory from 1954 to 1956, and whose family and ours had been close friends for over fifty years, invited Ginnie, Katie, and Meg to stay with him in his house. It was located in the lovely Newnham part of Cambridge near the Colleges, and Ginnie would be able to stay there until she found permanent housing. They descended on him that Saturday night, just over one day before Katie began her career at Hills Road.

The thought of joining Ginnie, and returning to Cambridge was irresistible. Just before Christmas of 2011, I flew to Boston, and then, joined by Kathy and my grandson John, we flew to England. Ginnie had arranged for a car to take us from Heathrow to Derbyshire, where several days before Christmas, we all met up at our cousins Sue and Gordon's marvelous B&B, which they turned over to us for the entire Christmas week.

Sue keeps a very comfortable set of bedrooms in a converted barn, each with its own luxurious bathroom. There is a kitchen on the ground floor from which Sue serves breakfast to her guests on tables in the sitting room. Outside in the barns are the animals the girls love, including an old dog and two younger ones, often with pups. Geese wander majestically about the farmyard, hissing at newcomers. There is a flower-filled garden close to the house, and the farmyard is noticeably neat: no discarded farm implements litter the land. Sue and Gordon's two sons live in houses on the farm, and work in partnership with their father; one daughter-in-law helps Sue, the other, who works as a veterinarian, is available whenever needed.

It was a happy and instructive time for Katie, who immediately joined the local Cambridge track-and-field team, and was soon running sprints and hurdling at a track a mile from our flat. She got into the social life quickly at Hills Road, as one of the several Americans. One teacher said she was a "breath of fresh air," with her outgoing Americanness and "can-do" spirit, but it didn't sit well with at least one teacher, who asked her if she were from Essex (Essex being the part of England where the equivalent of English Kardashians reputedly hail from.)

Katie joined the Hills Road soccer and volleyball team, made lots of friends, and soon was biking the several miles to school across the Cambridge Fens. For some reason (probably because no one in authority was alerted to the fact that she was American), Katie went along with her track team to compete in the British Nationals in Birmingham, running in a heat against a British Olympian, a great experience.

Unfortunately, the first months were a hell of homesickness for Meg. Four years earlier, Ginnie, Meg, and Kate had moved to our village in England, to test the waters for possibly moving the family to England permanently. (I happily joined them on this trip.) Meg ended up in a small Church of England village school, which went from "Reception" (four-year-olds) to age eleven. Ann Punchard, the head teacher, was a bundle of energy; warm, bright, always on the go. Ginnie said she was the best teacher she'd known—ever. Despite having to wear a school uniform, Meg thrived, although Kate's unhappiness at her school precipitated our return to America.

When we arrived this time, Ginnie had expected to put Meg into the local public school, as the daughter of a British citizen. But the laws had changed, and a private school was the only option. Meg chafed at the religious instruction, the daily religious all-school assembly, and the constricting school uniform. She was absolutely miserable, until six months into their time there, when

Katie and Meg were granted visas that allowed them "Leave for Indefinite Remain in the United Kingdom." Ginnie immediately switched Meg into the local state school, populated by the children of Cambridge academics and which was very similar to Meg's school back in Boston. Finally, Meg was happy, did well, and had many friends.

Ginnie spent weeks looking for places to live until a flat came available directly across from Mike Bown. Being so close to Mike pleased all of us greatly, as we were able to see a lot of each other, and he was always popping by with something he thought we could use. Soon, he was coming over for dinner many nights, bringing his own meal, which he much preferred to our fare. Nearby were walks through fields along the River Cam to the town center, and in the other direction to Grantchester where we walked or drove to take tea in the orchard as Joe and I had done when we lived there from 1954-1956, and on our annual visits to Cambridge especially when the girls were young.

At the weekends, we often drove up to Derbyshire where we stayed with Joe's cousins and the girls spent time with their cousins.

After a year at Hills Road, Katie decided she wanted her last year before college to be at her old high school. Meg was harder to displace from Cambridge because she was having a good time, was in the midst of the social whirl, and was doing well academically, but was happy to return to her American friends. I must say that, in July 2012, when Ginnie and I got on the bus at Parker's Piece in Cambridge that would take us to Heathrow Airport, we both had tears in our eyes for what we were leaving behind, and for what might have been.

After I returned with Ginnie and girls from England, I went to live with Sue and family for seven months where, as I have described in the Madison chapter, I enjoyed excellent theater in Spring Green, the local symphony where I met a great many of her friends, some of whom I now feel are mine. Sue and David are members of the C. S. Lewis Society of Madison that meets monthly to discuss all things Lewis, including his Narnia Chronicles. In 2012, the group held a conference at which ten Lewis scholars presented their work. Two years later, David and Susan coedited a book based on those lectures entitled *C. S. Lewis's List: The Ten Books That Influenced Him Most*, published by Bloomsbury Press. Susan's husband, David, is working as a faculty associate with Independent Learning at University of Wisconsin-Madison Extension. Their daughter, Jessica graduated from the University of Wisconsin-Madison, majoring in English and Theater, and recently married Noah, a systems engineer.

I now live with Ginnie and her family in Massachusetts, and I come home with her to England every summer, sometimes accompanied by one or two of her children. In Brookline, in addition to taking part in a memoir group each week and a mystery book club at the local library every month, I attend church with Ginnie in nearby Jamaica Plain, at an Episcopalian (Anglican) church and have many friends among that congregation. My granddaughter, Katie, graduated from Smith College last spring, worked for Senator Elizabeth Warren, and is pursuing a career in government or management consulting prior to graduate work. My grandson John, a junior at Eckerd College, is majoring in Spanish and History, and is enjoying his time in Florida. My youngest grandchild, Meg, is a high school freshman, with a particular interest in science. I have enjoyed following all of their various paths in life.

❦

I have been blessed with over fifty years of companionship of a brilliant, hardworking, multitalented, and loving husband, who took me to America—twice!—and then around the globe. I have seen the most glorious places on earth—the deserts, coasts, and mountains of the American West, the deserts of Australia, the lush tropics and volcanoes of Hawaii, the ice, volcanoes, and stark beauty of Iceland, the history and architectural wonders of Europe.

I have seen great progress in American society, from water fountains from which only white Americans could drink in the 1950s, to the ascension of a highly intelligent, inspiring, and far-sighted African American president.

I have made friends with people across the globe, from dear friends who lost most or all of their families in the Holocaust, to brilliant scientists and Nobel Prize winners of a world-class university.

I feel grateful for my years in America, a country I have come to love, and I am also grateful to be able to return home every summer with Ginnie to my village and family in the Peak District. Nothing will ever be as it was when Joe was with me, but I am so glad to have married him and shared our lives together. Now, with the love of my two daughters and my four grandchildren, I am a lucky woman.

Made in the USA
Middletown, DE
03 December 2022

15992641R00176